LEARNER MANAGED LEARNING

LEARNER MANAGED LEARNING

The key to lifelong learning and development

DOUGLAS G LONG

Kogan Page, London / St Martin's Press, New York

To my children as they progress in the adventure of lifelong learning

First published in 1990 in Great Britain by
Kogan Page Limited
120 Pentonville Road
London N1 9JN

British Library Cataloguing in Publication Data
A CIP record for this book is available from the British Library
ISBN (UK) 0 74940 339 X

First published in 1990 in the United States of America by
St Martin's Press Inc.,
175 Fifth Avenue, New York
NY 10010

Library of Congress Cataloging-in-Publication Data
A CIP record for this book is available from the Library of Congress
ISBN (USA) 0-312-06088-2

Printed and bound in Great Britain by Biddles Ltd, Guildford
Typeset by Selectmove Ltd, London

Self-Directed Learning is that process in which individuals take the initiative, with or without the help of others, in diagnosing their learning needs, formulating learning goals, identifying human and material resources for learning, choosing and implementing learning strategies, and evaluating learning outcomes.

Malcolm Knowles
1975

Contents

Preface

For some considerable time now the concept of self-directed learning has received at least lip-service from educators and trainers. Perhaps the best definition of the phrase is that made by Malcolm Knowles in the quotation which precedes this introduction. Unfortunately it appears to me as though the term has been debased by a popularist concept which implies that if a learner has some input as to the learning process then self-directed learning can occur. On the other hand there are people who oppose the concept on the grounds that while it may encourage greater commitment to personal development, it is inappropriate for the 'hard science' areas or the development even of such skills as writing and reading.

In this book I have endeavoured to provide a different perspective. It is now almost twenty years since my interest and involvement in learner managed learning commenced. In that time I have gained experience in using the concept, not only from a personal perspective but also in universities, industry, and commerce in Australia, New Zealand, the United States of America, and South-East Asia. I have incorporated within this book brief case studies and anecdotes drawn from that experience. The examples used are of people ranging from teenagers through to people in their mid to late 50s. They encompass a broad range of prior qualifications, experience, and interests while the nationalities of these people are as varied as those in the three continents in which they live.

In choosing examples and case studies I have been mindful of the fact that the readers of this book will not only be those in the normal educational spheres of schools and universities, but also those involved in human resource development activities in both the for-profit and not-for-profit employment sectors. The point I seek to make is that learner managed learning is applicable across the full spectrum of human experience.

Throughout the book I refer extensively to other writers who, both directly and indirectly, speak of issues that impact on learner managed learning. In some instances I have chosen to use direct quotations and diagrams or figures developed by these people. In other instances I have paraphrased their words so as to encapsulate the meaning of their arguments. I believe that all such references are cited and every effort has been made to ensure acknowledgement is given. My debt to these people who have helped mould my own thoughts is immense and, hopefully, for those who wish to engage in further in-depth study of learner managed learning the bibliography will provide a good 'jumping off point.' Those whose interest is more in obtaining a basic understanding of the issues relating to learner managed learning will be able to do so without extensive recourse to the bibliography but with the security of knowing the issues are well researched and supported.

The book has changed from talking of self-directed learning to talking of 'learner managed learning'. The key emphasis that I seek to make is that for lifelong learning to become a reality in any person's experience it is necessary for them to be active in controlling their entire learning process. The one constant I have found in every case centres on willingness and ability to take responsibility for managing one's own learning experience. When this is done then the entire educational experience, whether through formal or informal programmes in the workplace, in the normal formal educational context, or elsewhere, becomes exciting and positive. It enables us to deal with many of the problems faced in relation to drop-outs, discipline, and apathy. It also means significantly harder work for those involved in facilitating the learning process and will not appeal to those who see teaching or training as being a soft option in the employment sphere.

My experience is that the effort is worth it. The sense of personal and professional satisfaction one feels as one watches this growth towards individual responsibility and a hunger for growth and development is immense. To see a person blossom towards personal fulfilment, from frustration and mediocrity in the workplace because they were unable or unwilling to learn while at school is, in my experience, one of the greatest rewards those involved in adult education can receive.

This book has evolved over a period of years. In January 1986 while visiting the United States of America and discussing the work with which I was involved it was suggested that the School of Public Administration at University of Southern California would be interested in hearing of my work and, perhaps, having it included as part of their International Training of Trainers Programme. The first draft of this book arose out of my preparation for the

International Training of Trainers Programme held in July/August 1986.

As I researched learner managed learning it became apparent that there were many writers on the subject and many case studies yet there was very little available that sought to draw together the various strands and to present a unified whole. Works seemed to be oriented either to those wishing to implement learner managed learning or to those wishing to undertake learner managed learning. It is this issue of drawing various strands together that is attempted within this book. I have sought to show how the work of various writers meshes together and, by coupling that with experience and examples, I have sought to show that learner managed learning is a key ingredient for organisational and personal growth. Accordingly the opening chapters examine current approaches to education and learning together with looking at a rationale for learner managed learning. This section is rounded off in Chapter 8 where I present a model for learner managed learning and, from there on, move to looking at how it can be implemented. The intention is that this book will prove useful both to the individual wishing to undergo learner managed learning experiences and to organisations or individuals who wish to implement learner managed learning or assist others in the implementation of learner managed learning.

Learner managed learning is not a panacea for all training or educational ills, nor does it appear to be something which every individual will want to embrace. It is, however, amongst the most powerful tools available for educators. It has application in every walk of life and with any person who is genuinely interested in taking responsibility for their own growth and development.

There is still much work to be done. I believe that there needs to be a broad exchange of information about learner managed learning programmes and the experience that people have with this concept. There is a need for further research as to the long-term academic and professional development of people who have embraced learner managed learning as well as research into the extent to which learner managed learning in one area of life has impacted on all areas of an individual's life. This book is but one step in such a quest and, hopefully, it will provide an impetus for others to explore these and other areas.

I must express my gratitude to various colleagues in the United States and within Australia who have helped me in regard to this project. Some, such as Irv Rubin of Honolulu and Peter Peterson of Sydney have taken the trouble to search out and provide me with relevant material that I may not otherwise have discovered.

Others have taken the trouble to read my early manuscripts and to provide comment and ask questions. This has added considerably to the final version. Five colleagues particularly have worked closely in various stages of the development of this manuscript. To Ian Reid I owe a tremendous debt for his critical assessment and suggestions but, in recognising Ian's contribution, it is important also to thank Merinda Air, Lesley DiLaudo, Mariane Ford, and Harald Wellenberg for their encouragement, support, and extremely hard work in so many different areas of the development of this work.

Douglas G Long
Sydney
July 1990

1   A Lifetime of Learning

Case study: *Quo Vadis?*

In his early 50s, approaching the end of his career as a police officer, Arthur was facing the vexed question of what to do when he retired. On leaving school he had served an apprenticeship within the motor industry prior to joining the police department when aged 20. In those days requirements were for physical fitness and a willingness to learn policing from the perspective of a practitioner rather than attendance at a police academy. Most of his training had been done on the job with the formal training relating to fundamentals of law, use of firearms, and an introduction to policing occurring in a two-week period of orientation.

Over the years Arthur had seen considerable changes and, in the main, he believed these were for the better. He had seen the training of recruits develop to a high level and he had seen the training of sergeants and commissioned officers become an essential part of the promotion process. For the past five years he had been a senior member of the team responsible for training detectives and he assisted in training in other areas. Increasingly he had realised his own need for further education and qualifications.

Several years ago, as the result of an injury received in the course of his duty, Arthur had needed to receive chiropractic treatment. Over a period of weeks he had come to learn what was involved in qualifying as a chiropractor and, from the relief he had received, he believed that the services provided by chiropractors were both valuable and in demand. Arthur applied for, was accepted, and embarked upon a period of training. The police department allowed him to do this on a part-time basis.

The experience of being involved in formal education whetted Arthur's appetite. In 1987 when he approached me for some advice he was looking for ways in which he could further his general knowledge and, without adversely impacting on his day to day work, obtain qualifications that would stand him in good stead as he moved into the third phase of his working career – the post-police period. He was enthusiastic about formal learning; he had undoubted ability to assimilate knowledge; and he was realistic in the availability of time and financial resources to put into such a course of study. A programme leading to a Bachelor's Degree from one of Australia's newer universities was the obvious choice and, as this institution advocated learner managed learning approaches, Arthur was encouraged to submit an application. He was accepted, and in 1989, he commenced a course of study, using learner managed learning principles, that would ensure his post-police period would be entered with formal qualifications in adult education and training.

Learning and change

Throughout the ages, probably the most crucial issue that has faced humanity is that of change. The increasing complexity of this change throughout the 20th century has come from a virtually exponential growth in knowledge and technology so that, as has been said often, we no longer die in the same world into which we were born. Experience indicates that change occurs so rapidly that, for most people, it is necessary to have two, three, or more career changes in a normal work life of thirty to forty years. It has been said that the half life of most professional knowledge is less than five years. This creates problems that are vastly different in magnitude from those experienced by our forefathers. Many of us experience considerable difficulty dealing with this change and, in such instances, dilemmas like that faced by Arthur when in his early 50s are not uncommon. The difference between Arthur and many others who face the same issue, is that Arthur was willing to take responsibility for managing the change he was encountering rather than stagnating or simply accepting the inevitability of retirement followed by a void.

The issue of change and our need for managing this has been addressed across a broad spectrum by people such as Peccei (1979), Toffler (1970 and 1981), Bennis (1985), through to Peters (1987) and others. All have considered the issue of change and all have suggested ways in which we can manage change. Perhaps, however, the key to the issue is summarised by Peccei (1979: XIV-XVI) '. . . what we all need at this point in human evolution is to learn what it takes to learn what we should learn – and learn it.'

What is learning? Despite all of the evidence around us and the literature with which we are bombarded it still appears as though, in too many quarters, either learning is equated with education or is seen as being in competition to education. Either of these extremes results in a situation in which education is pursued as an end on its own or formal education is ridiculed as being irrelevant and, in fact, an impediment to the real business of living. Although such polarity occurs rarely, some degree of confusion between the two seems to occur amongst most of the people with whom I discuss the issue.

Again, this problem is not new. Stones (1966), Botkin, Elmadjra and Malitza (1979), and Nadler (1982) are but a few of those who have grappled with the distinction in concepts between the two. Stones (1966: 51) talks of 'the naive idea' of learning being that which happens to the pupil when a teacher is instructing. He sees this as being inadequate and misleading as it assumes a restriction on the use of the term and assumes that the dispensing of information by the teacher necessarily involves its assimilation by the taught. From here he goes on to look at learning as occurring throughout the entire life cycle for both positive and negative results. He instances rehabilitation after a serious injury, addiction to drugs, and criminal behaviour as all involving aspects of learning. This leads him to the emphasis of learning as being an active process and he concludes '. . . we cannot say that learning has taken place until we can observe in some way the changes in the behaviour of the animal or person, brought about by learning.'

Botkin, Elmadjra and Malitza (1979: 8) stress learning as an approach both to knowledge and to life that emphasises human initiative. They see it as the process of preparing to deal with new situation and as occurring both consciously and unconsciously from experiencing real-life situations. Their concern is for the inadequacy of learning processes which lag appallingly behind societal needs and are leaving both individuals and societies unprepared to meet the challenges posed by global issues. In their eyes the failure of learning processes means that, all too often, human preparedness remains under-developed on a world-wide scale. The result is, in their view, that human potential is being artificially constrained and vastly under-utilised. It is this that leads them to conclude that '. . . for all practical purposes there appear to be virtually no limits to learning.'

Nadler (1982: 2) provides a further overview when he talks of the difference between experience (or incidental learning) and education (or intentional learning). He talks of behaviour or performance as being the sum of experience and education less the effect of any filtering done by our culture and personality. From here he goes on to speak of learning as being something which occurs independently of any structured or programmed learning activity while stressing that education provides both a framework within which we can maximise the benefit of experience and a control that can minimise the possibility of 'remaking the wheel' or replicating mistakes previously made. He develops this further as a means by which professionals can keep up-to-date in their field and, (Nadler and Wiggs (1986: 161)) expands this by talking of experience and education being combined in the activity of learner managed learning – an activity seen as being essential for total growth and development.

In order to minimise the possibility of confusion, I am using the definition of learning provided by Zimbardo (1979: 63) as a working definition. Zimbardo defines learning as 'a relatively permanent change in behaviour as a result of experience.' This definition allows for a balance between intentional learning and incidental learning but moves beyond the acquisition of knowledge to the stage where such knowledge impacts on behaviour. It is the sort of learning that is illustrated in the case of Arthur. Arthur's experience showed very clearly that police officers who retired without having prepared themselves for the post-police period found their options extremely limited. This experience led him to undertake further studies and the combination of both of these meant that both his present behaviour was experiencing change and this process would be continuing into his retirement cycle of life.

Learning theories

Although there may be confusion amongst the general population as to the relationship between learning and education the whole area is one which has received considerable study over the years. This has resulted in several key approaches being propounded. The stimulus response work of Pavlov (1927) and Thorndyke (1905) led to the behavioural work epitomised by Skinner (1938, 1971, 1974) while cognitive theories from people such as Tolman (1949) and social learning (Bandura (1977), Bandura and Walter (1959)), have all had their advocates and detractors. The thing which appears to be common amongst all the writers in the field is that learning is not considered to have taken place unless that learning exhibits itself in an aspect of behaviour. Consistently the point is made that the only way in which the extent of learning can be assessed is by observing the actual behaviours of subjects rather than relying on written or verbal affirmations of what could or should occur in any given situation. It is this which has led writers as diverse as Merrill and Reid (1981) and Byrd and Moore (1982) to examine the applications of learning in such fields as interpersonal relationships or decision making. The emphasis of these writers is that we obtain a perception of the learning a person has experienced by the behaviour we see that person exhibiting.

On the other hand, education can be assessed differently. If we provide a pre-test in relation to the knowledge a person currently has about a particular topic then provide a series of lectures, readings, audio-visual presentations, or some other educational means, and follow that by a post-test it is possible to measure any change in awareness about that topic. Whether or not that change in awareness impacts on a change in behaviour is a second question. Hersey and

Blanchard (1988: 4) make a very clear distinction between knowledge, attitudes, individual behaviour, and group behaviour and stress that a change in knowledge and/or a change in group behaviour does not necessarily mean that the knowledge has been internalised and is being exhibited when an individual is on their own.

An anecdote illustrates this fact. A colleague who was involved in the educational rehabilitation process of drink drivers tells of classes in which persons convicted of drink driving were subjected to experiences designed to make them aware of the dangers of alcohol. They would hear lectures and see films that impressed upon them the tragic outcomes possible from combining alcohol with driving a motor vehicle. The result was that, as they left the auditorium they were the most careful drivers in the world yet the instance of people returning following further convictions was demoralisingly high. In this instance education had occurred but learning in the sense of education being translated into behaviour was not evidenced. It became very clear to my colleague that if learning was to occur then the individuals needed to take responsibility for the learning process and to have a personal commitment to the outcomes of any educational processes undergone.

Dewsbury (1984: 240) summarises research as far back as 1910 which indicates that there is little evidence of consistent, meaningful differences between species in the rate of learning to handle different problems. Rather there is quite clear difference in learning rates between specific animals or individuals. In other words, the rate of assimilation of knowledge differs not between cats and dogs, people and monkeys, or any other animal group but is unique to each particular subject studied. Despite all the research which supports this contention it would appear as though our educational institutions tend to acknowledge such differences more in theory than in fact. Part of the reason for this is economic – the cost of seeking to determine a particular learning programme for every student at every level in our educational system is prohibitive. Part of the reason also lies in the application of statistics and averaging in which we are able to gauge with a reasonably high degree of accuracy that an educational experience geared to a particular level will ensure the vast majority of students acquire the minimum level of education determined by our various systems. It remains a fact, however, that we are ill-equipped in general to deal with those individuals who fall on either extreme of the normal curve by having either learning difficulties or experiencing boredom because the learning experience is not moving at an adequate rate.

Learning theories and learner managed learning

Learner managed learning is a process which seeks to address this problem. With the application of learner managed learning principles (see Chapters 4–8) it becomes possible to tailor a learning experience to suit the rate of assimilation of the student. In so doing the concept seeks to pay close attention to learning research and to apply such research in every-day learning experiences.

The work of Pavlov, Thorndyke, Skinner, and the like has been criticised on the grounds that it tends to be manipulative and can lead to extremes such as brainwashing and aversion therapy. The works of people such as Tolman, Bandura, Walter, and others has received the criticism that individual responsibility is removed from the learning process either by our genetic predisposition or the environment which impacts upon us. While it is true that there are negative aspects and shortcomings to most theories and it is also true that even the most valuable tool can be abused, it is important that we do not lose the positive insights provided by writers such as these. Each can support the viewpoint they propound by both research and observation. Question may arise as to the research methodology and as to the ethics of certain areas of research but, in general, it must be admitted that the whole field of learning is a complex one in which each of these writers has made a contribution.

Learner managed learning seeks to create a situation in which common themes from the learning theorists can be coupled with individual responsibility in such a way that the educator becomes a facilitator within the learning process. Worell and Nelson (1974: 3) advocate the educator as becoming a partner in facilitating new ways for people to learn important skills through the obtaining of maximum approval and reinforcement. They see the need for the learner to apply a self-reinforcement system to the effective maintenance of his or her own behaviour through the setting of realistic goals, supply of appropriate self-instructions, and providing his or her own positive and negative consequences in order to inhibit or produce behaviour. The ability to apply such self-reinforcement system they see as being evidence of a person having developed the capability required for self-control. As they point out, the eventual aim of all educators must be to move any child gradually away from external control processes towards internalised control. In learner managed learning we are trying to extend this a little further by getting the learner to take responsibility not only for controlling their learning process but also for determining the education process that is required for their overall growth and development.

The issue of reinforcement is important. One of the criticisms often put forward against the stimulus response concept and the whole process of behavioural modification is that it is manipulative. Eysenck (1965) looks at the difference between many of the claims made for the application of psychological processes and the fact of what changes psychological processes can bring. In this he discusses examples of behaviour modification by positive and negative reinforcement with little attention to what is or should be accepted. It is only of relatively recent days that ethical considerations relating to these have received extensive publicity. Many of the experiments and exercises that were carried out in the 20s, 30s, 40s, 50s and even the 60s would today be totally prohibited on ethical grounds. Worell and Nelson (1974: 3) are among many who have addressed this issue in the past twenty or so years. They conclude that learning which seeks to increase the self-esteem and self-discipline of each individual uses acceptable procedures even though extrinsic reinforcement may be used. It becomes quite clear that there is a world of difference between unethical, manipulative behaviour which benefits only the person providing reinforcement and a system of reinforcement that moves an individual to self-sufficiency and independence. This is not to say that the end justifies the means. What it is saying is that in seeking to help a person experience growth in self-esteem, self-discipline, and independence, the means and the end are equally important and involve a careful consideration of the requirements of each person involved. It is this positive application of reinforcement (be it extrinsic or intrinsic) that is used by learner managed learning as it promotes self-sufficiency and independence.

Adult learning

In Chapter 4 the issue of adult learning compared with teaching of children (andragogy vs. pedagogy) will be examined and the argument will be made that many of the problems we experience with our existing approach to education and learning are caused because the emphasis tends to be upon pedagogy rather than andragogy. In the vast majority of cases, little or no attempt is made to find a balance between two extremes. The result is, as already stated, one in which large numbers of people see education as being irrelevant and opt out of developing themselves while, at the same time, discouraging other people from undertaking further education and learning.

This situation must change. In today's world everyone is threatened when intellectual stagnation occurs. In countries where the social responsibility insists that those who are unable to contribute to the economy by their work must be cared for by the state it is obvious that any inability to generate income because of inadequate knowledge and skills affects not only the individual but the rest of society. In a somewhat less obvious way the same is true in countries that do not have such a concept of social responsibility. In these countries there can tend to be a rise in anti-social activities such as crime, begging, and general dehumanising of individuals. In light of the fact that productivity is related to morale, anything which tends to lower national or individual morale (whether of nationals or of people outside that nation) in regards to the economy, must have a deleterious effect.

Learner managed learning is a means by which these deficiencies can be remedied. If we are encouraging individuals to take responsibility, throughout their life, for their own learning process, we have gone a long way towards alleviating the problems of human obsolescence. In this concept the growth of individuals is encouraged so that they are better equipped to cope with the changing environment and to take increasing responsibility for their own destiny. Obviously there are problems and risks associated with this. Despite this, as is set out below, the problems and risks associated with lifelong learning and learner managed learning are significantly less than those associated with the traditional approaches that have been tried and are now found largely to be wanting.

Part of the difficulties relating to traditional learning approaches relate to the difference between what Botkin, Elmadjra and Malitza (1979: 10) call 'maintenance learning' and 'innovative learning'. They argue that the emphasis of our traditional learning is on the acquisition of fixed outlooks, methods, and rules for dealing with known and recurring situations. We seek to enhance problem-solving abilities for problems that are given and, by so doing, promote a type of learning designed to maintain an existing system or an established way of life. While acknowledging that there is and will continue to be a need for this type of learning they go on to advocate an approach which prepares people for a critical assessment of the overall implications from any experience. They argue that only such a change in emphasis will enable us to cope with increasing global complexity and change. They see humanity persistently lagging behind events and, accordingly, being subjected to whims of crisis. Until our learning experiences emphasise an innovative, pro-active approach, they question whether humanity can learn to guide its own destiny or whether events and crises will determine human conditions.

Botkin, Elmadjra and Malitza (1979: 12) describe innovative learning as involving anticipation. They see it as preparing people to use techniques such as forecasting, simulations, scenarios, and models so that they will consider trends and make plans to evaluate future consequences and possible injurious side-effects of present decisions. The aim of such an approach is to shield society from the trauma of learning by shock. It emphasises the future-tense not just the past: while employing imagination, it is based on hard fact.

One of the major international economic and analysis organisations in the world is the Club of Rome. In 1972 it prepared a report on educational issues (Botkin, Elmadjra and Malitza (1979)). While it is true that, since the publication of the Club of Rome Report, there has been a shift towards such an innovative learning approach, it is also true that our mainstream educational processes seem to concentrate still on maintenance rather than innovative learning. Where a move to innovative learning is encouraged there is all too often an emphasis on the rights for participation in determining the future of our planet but a reluctance to accept responsibility for the side-effects of change. The Club of Rome Report stresses that innovative learning requires individuals to accept participation in the sense of co-operation, dialogue, and empathy with open communication and the constant testing of one's operating rules and values. Alongside of this, however, lies a responsibility towards not only those who are supportive of change but those who are adversely affected by it and, accordingly, resistant to it.

Toffler (1986: 11) argues that all industrial societies develop systems of mass education. Although, on the surface, there may be differences in education systems in various countries – particularly if one looks at the visible curriculum – in fact the covert curriculum shows startling similarities. He argues that virtually all children in all the industrial societies study three fundamental hidden courses. These courses are in punctuality, obedience, and in rote and repetitive work. We teach these courses by requiring children to show up on time and to be in appropriate places when the bell rings or the designated starting time for any class is otherwise indicated. Obedience is taught because, even in the places where they are encouraged to ask questions, the smart ones know which ones you don't ask. The emphasis of our teaching system is on the pupil accepting the authority of the teacher in terms of content and process. Rote and repetitive work is taught by the normal exposure children receive year after year in terms of being able to remember and repeat data for the purpose of examination.

The reason for this, according to Toffler, is that all industrial societies rely on certain fundamental principles and engage in standardisation. They seek to produce entrants to the work force who approximate some form of procrustean bed because it is easier to deal with people who conform than it is to deal with eccentrics and mavericks who, perhaps, question whether the norm to which conformity is required is really a valid norm. This is seen in the value systems reflected when teachers, trainers and professors discuss their students and, very often, when members of the general public comment on the behaviour of students. It is seen also in managers speaking of employees. A 'good' student or employee is one who gives due respect to the person in authority and evidences this respect by, all too often, docile obedience rather than questioning or seeking discussion about the rights and wrongs of such actions. The Nuremberg trials made it clear that a defence of following orders was inadequate against charges of war crimes. Despite this virtually every nation through its educational processes seems to encourage behaviour in which obedience to authority is accepted as mandatory. We encourage a reliance upon positional power (see Chapter 6) and then wonder why this power is either abused or ignored.

Boyer (1987) in examining the undergraduate experience in American colleges and universities adds support to Toffler's contentions. He says (page 283) 'throughout our study we were impressed that what today's college is teaching most successfully is competence – competence in meeting schedules, in gathering information, in responding well on tests, in mastering the details of a special field. Today the capacity to deal successfully with discrete problem is highly prized. And when we asked students about their education, they, almost without exception, spoke about the credits they had earned or the courses they still needed to complete.' Boyer sees that much of the emphasis of our educational system has been on preparing people for the work-place rather than encouraging them to learn. We have concentrated on maintenance learning rather than on innovative learning.

Toffler argues that today we should be moving beyond this sort of approach because we are moving towards a new civilisation with its own new systems. He sees this as being not merely a straight line extension of the old industrial civilisation but, in fact, based on new technologies and new principles which may well be in conflict with past technologies and principles. He sees this as having impact on our social structures as well as every other aspect of life. It is his belief that we should be developing people who are able to cope with the complexities of these changes and, in fact, to assist in the overall development of this new society and structure into which we are moving. In the Club of Rome terms, Toffler would argue that we must be encouraging innovative learning rather than simply maintenance learning. Only an innovative learning concept will enable the transition to a third wave society.

Again Boyer's research enforces this idea. On page 276 he says:

> There is one additional point to be underscored. Most college graduates – both minority and non-minority – will not seek advanced degrees. They should, however, both as workers and members of their community go on learning long after college days are over. If the college is the institution of the book and a place that cherishes ideas, criticism, and creativity, the graduate of the college will continue to read and think, study, and reflect throughout life. Without continued learning, graduates will lose both their intellectual vitality and their capacity effectively to serve.
>
> If the undergraduate college has succeeded, students, after they are handed their diplomas, will be well equipped to put their work in context and move with success from one intellectual challenge to another. More than that, they should be able to see their jobs in larger perspective. Only then can they be truly creative and fulfilled as individuals.

All of this means that the emphasis is shifting away from a pedagogical approach to an andragogical approach. This is not only in terms of teaching methodology but also of teaching emphasis. It requires our teaching to be problem-centred insofar as people recognise problems are occurring and then seek strategies and learning that will enable them to meet and deal with these problems. In this regard they will need a facilitator rather than a teacher so that they can take an increasing responsibility for the meeting of these problems and for their entire individual growth process. That this challenges the status quo is a given and, for this reason, the issue of learner managed learning and power will be discussed in Chapter 6 and the issue of problems associated with learner managed learning will be discussed in Chapter 13.

In the earlier example of Arthur we have an example of a popularist concept of innovative learning. Arthur's situation and studies met many of the requirements of adult learning insofar as they were problem-centred and sought to deal with a future situation. However, it lacked the full concept of innovative learning as proposed by the Club of Rome as there was not the possibility for Arthur to have participation within the entire police training system to the end that all police officers would be encouraged to examine the experience of police officers who had retired and consider the implications of this both for themselves and for the department as a whole. Arthur, although willing to participate with the police department in this regard, was unable to do so because of the very nature of the system within which he worked.

The change towards innovative, adult learning is coming and many exciting steps have been taken. Despite this, we are still at the stage of learning '. . . what it takes to learn what we should learn – and learn it.'

2   Recurrent Education

Case study: *One by ten or ten by one?*

Barbara is a senior executive in a financial institution. She is 35 years old and her qualifications include an MBA from one of the top schools in the country. Prior to taking up her present position she had worked in a government department where her rapid promotion on merit meant that she attracted the attention of executive search companies acting on behalf of private sector organisations. That was five years ago. Now things seem to have ground to a halt. The last five years have seen only one promotion and Barbara is becoming increasingly frustrated at the failure of her present employer fully to utilise her skills.

The last three years have seen Barbara back at school. She has sought out educational and training programmes designed to upgrade her knowledge and skills in areas relevant to her work environment. She is aware of areas of knowledge necessary at the top of her company but in which she is lacking and she has taken steps to deal with such deficiencies. Accordingly she has done a Graduate Diploma in Organisation behaviour as well as various short courses dealing with human resources management and interpersonal relations. These do not seem to have enhanced her career prospects with her present employer and now, as well as looking at on-going educational requirements, she is considering other career prospects.

The limitations of relevance

I am not sure where I read it or heard it but, several years ago, the statement was made that the 'half-life of any education today is around five years.' In context the argument was being made that there is a limited relevance in what we teach. The frontiers of knowledge are expanding so rapidly and so widely that each of us can absorb only a fraction of what is available and, in many instances, the gap between new discoveries and their implementation is such that we are constantly implementing obsolete technologies and concepts. This does not mean that we are necessarily tardy in implementing new knowledge. Rather it means that, all too often, knowledge is advancing faster than it is possible to implement it even when that implementation is fast tracked and streamlined. Under these circumstances there is an understandable cynicism in many quarters about what is taught in our educational systems.

Kramer (1986) raises the issues of what she entitles 'the tyranny of relevance' by explaining that relevance, at the moment, means what is up-to-date, topical, controversial, expedient, entertaining, and utilitarian. She argues that trivial relevance of this kind has now become the central principle governing educational policy. The question asked by many educationists is first, 'what is relevant to students' interests?' not 'what do students need?' She sees the word 'need' as taken to signify only the narrowest view of the usefulness of schooling as this is defined in terms of its immediate short-term relevance. She sees the common notion as being that what a student needs is what is relevant to specific employment and so needs become what the market place dictates and what society appears to require.

Kramer is strongly critical of this short-sighted view of relevance in curriculum. She says:

> Such curriculum while it appears to offer choices, in fact is narrowly prescriptive, by catering for the existing, rather than the potential interests of students on the one hand, and on the other for the supposed needs and requirements of society. In short it proposes restricting the educational experience of students by endorsing a facile notion of relevance which does not recognise the distinction between education and training.
>
> The dreary functionalism of this view of education is supported by a large, and possibly growing, number of educators, educational administrators, and politicians.

Kramer is a classics scholar and, perhaps understandably, argues for a broad grounding in the classics as providing a foundation on which people can build using their understanding of history, logic, and the like which are to be found therein. While not everyone would agree with Kramer's call for a classical education, there is widespread concern as to the relevance of what we teach people whether it be in schools, universities and colleges, or in the work place. In his study of the American educational system Boyer (1987) makes comments which echo the sentiments from Kramer. His research showed that some observers questioned the value of a liberal education on the grounds that liberal arts majors typically have not been able to secure employment before they graduate. The result is that, while marking time, they often take a blue collar or pink collar job for which they may be over-qualified. Boyer finds, however, that long-term prospects are much brighter. He quotes a University of Illinois survey regarding the success of its graduates in finding jobs. This study revealed that although liberal arts graduates may have a tougher time immediately after graduation they closed the gap over time. He goes on to say (page 269):

> Further, liberal arts alumni tend to be satisfied with their education. This was typical of the comments received: 'College didn't fit me for any certain career, but it taught me how to learn.'

Boyer contrasts this with the colleges and universities that, in his terms, have tended to become training departments for industry and commerce rather than equipping people for the real business of living and dealing with the challenges of everyday life.

In May 1984 the Centre for Continuing Education of the Australian National University published a paper called *Recurrent Education for Australia: Statement of Intent*. In this paper they discussed the ways in which the personal, familial, communal, and occupational learning needs of people change at different stages during their lives and the way in which the educational system must be geared to meet these needs. The paper draws heavily on the OECD report *Recurrent Education* (OECD, Paris 1973) and describes recurrent education as an interrelated set of policies and strategies aimed at promoting re-allocation of educational opportunities in such a way that education will be available to people throughout life on a recurring or alternating basis, tailored to the various needs of individuals and groups. The OECD report talks of such education being centred on formal, accredited institutions but sees an important adjunct to this lying in various forms of deliberately arranged, non-formal, education and training, both public and private. The Centre for Continuing Education, while not advocating a parallel, rival, or compensatory system alongside the existing formal, accredited institutions, provides evidence of a concern in educational circles that the existing approaches are not meeting the total needs of society. The fact of this paper being propounded by a body such as the Centre for Continuing Education indicates that there is a dissatisfaction with existing educational processes and shows a willingness to investigate other approaches. There is a need, however, for a perspective that is outside of the traditional educational system. In Australia this is currently met by bodies such as the Australian Institute of Management, various professional bodies, consultants, and the like. The standards of material and education vary widely and there is a dearth of objective information generally available as to the standard of each such offering. Consequently, although recurring education is certainly available, to those seeking it there is a similarity with playing Russian roulette. Very often there has been a period of some years between one educational experience and the next so that learners are out of touch both with current offerings and the suitability of any such offering to their particular learning need.

It is quite apparent that although the availability of recurrent education is essential there is much to be said for an approach which enables the linkage of education in such a way as to minimise its weaknesses and maximise its benefits. Such an approach is to be found in the concept of lifelong learning.

Lifelong learning

There is more than just a semantic difference between 'recurrent education' and 'lifelong learning'. The general consensus regarding recurrent education appears to be that recurrent education is development which is provided from within the existing educational framework. Lifelong learning is not necessary within that framework. As Nadler (1982:2) says, it takes into account the incidental and the intentional aspects of learning.

The concept of lifelong learning argues that the process of learning ought to continue throughout an individual's life, whether or not there is involvement with the formal educational system. It recognises that much of the learning people do will take place outside of any formal or recognised educational system. This does not imply that an individual will always realise that a learning experience is occurring. Although Stones (1966:51) stresses learning must be considered as 'an active process' it is quite clear that this active process is very often more an aspect of experience rather than an intentional desire to undergo an education. What lifelong learning seeks to do is to provide a framework within which an individual can reflect on the past and prepare for the future in terms of learning experiences. It seeks to alert individuals both to their environment and to the growth potential from every experience. In so doing it includes recurrent education but it is not limited to formal educational experiences.

Virtually all psychologists, anthropologists, and other learning theorists describe patterns of learning that occur within the animal species. Most learning theory appears to be based on our observations from experiments with animals. That this has led to abuses and questionably ethical experimentation is commented upon in Chapter 1. In order to prove a theory there have been researchers who have submitted animals to intolerable conditions of pain and manipulation. The ability to understand what is occurring and to be pro-active in selecting learning experiences is one of the key factors that differentiates humanity from the lower species of animals. We have the power to choose, to understand, and to extrapolate observation and experience into theory and model.

Koestler (1975) is especially critical of this reliance upon bird and animal research and extrapolations made from this for human behaviour. He discusses what he calls 'the philosophy of ratomorphism' which he sees as having replaced the anthropomorphic fallacy (ascribing to animals human facilities and sentiments) with the opposite fallacy – denying man's faculties not found in lower animals. He sees this as a kind of flat earth view of the mind which 'has substituted for the erstwhile anthropomorphic view of the rat, a ratomorphic view of man.' His argument is that we should recognise the contributions made by the behaviourists in terms of recognising that we get what we reward rather than necessarily getting what we want in terms of performance be it academic, social, or employment. At the same time, however, he shows how essential it is to recognise the complexity of the human being and to ensure that we study healthy humans and their learning processes rather than excessive reliance on experimentation with animals. When we do this it becomes clear that cognitive aspects of learning are very real and that, very often, our development is geared not by reinforcement theory but by a creativity urged to bring about a dream or a concept.

Agor (1986) in discussing the role of intuition in decision making moves beyond the pure behaviourist approach. In discussing field studies on the use of intuition among managers (in the first study over 2,000 managers were tested using selected questions from the Myers Briggs Type Indicator while during 1984 a major follow-up study was conducted amongst those top executives who had scored in the top 10 per cent on the intuition scale) he says that respondents emphasised intuition as a key management resource that should be used to help guide strategic decisions. Many top executives stressed that good intuitive decisions were, in part, based on input from facts and experience gained over the years, combined and integrated with a well honed sensitivity or openness to other, more unconscious processes. In other words learning for these people embraced not just reinforcement from past experience or the input of academic education. The innovative concept of learning was important and impacted significantly on the way in which these executives made their decisions and achieved their goals. Agor points out that intuition was only one tool of many that they used in making their decisions but he does stress that it was and is an important tool that moves beyond the concept of maintenance learning or reinforcement theory as central to the development process.

Understanding and ability to conceptualise is a key factor in the overall development of individuals.

Not everyone uses this facility of understanding to the same extent. This is an issue addressed by Maslow (1968) when he talks in terms of 'deficiency motivation and growth motivation'. Maslow contended that most psychologists based their theories and observations on people who were experiencing difficulties rather than those who were healthy. Accordingly he saw the drives from such people as being those which met the deficiency needs and simply helped restore a person to a level of health and stability rather than impelling them forward through growth. He contended that only those persons whose main emphasis was towards self-actualisation would be those who would experience growth and development. When this is applied to learner managed learning it would appear as though those who are most likely to take responsibility for their own growth and development will be those who are driven by the self-actualisation need rather than the lower needs posited by Maslow in his hierarchy. This has implications for corporate human resource development and will be developed further in Chapters 10, 13, and 14. Maslow, however, certainly helps us to understand why there is so much emphasis on maintenance learning rather than innovative learning. If, as Maslow implies, the majority of emphasis is on dealing with people who are experiencing deficiency motivation then we are naturally going to be providing maintenance learning as a means to meet this deficiency rather than innovative learning which would be appropriate for those experiencing growth motivation. This will be considered further in Chapter 7.

Experiential learning

The other issue that requires attention at this stage is that of experiential learning. Again this will be explored in more detail in Chapter 5 but, as an initial comment, it must be noted that experiential learning is only one aspect of the lifelong learning process. Indeed, experience and activity without feedback and evaluation may not result in any learning at all. This certainly occurs when we repeat mistakes. It has been said that there is a vast difference between a person having ten years experience and one year's experience ten times. That difference is primarily the experiential learning that has occurred. The person who has undergone ten years experience has been through a growth process in which, either consciously or unconsciously, feedback and evaluation has occurred with the result that change has been implemented. The person having one year's experience ten times may have had identical experiences but has not processed these in terms of evaluation and feedback so that the need for change and the means of change have not become apparent and are not implemented. It is important to note, though, that adult learning takes full cognisance of the role of experience and seeks to build on this.

It is this that prompts Knowles (1970:37) to draw a distinction between the learning process for adults and that for children. He refers extensively to Alfred North Whitehead who, as early as 1931, was arguing for a change in the approach to the teaching of adults from that which was used to teach children. Knowles argues very strongly for the concept of lifelong learning to be instilled in children from a very early stage in their formal education. In this regard he reflects the emphasis of Maslow by implying that learning which is based on enabling people to meet their deficiency motivation needs is inadequate for the total development of an individual as a person in his or her own right.

In all the discussion so far the role of teachers has not been fully explored. Worell and Nelson (1974:3) and Knowles (1970:162) argue that the role of a teacher must be re-defined in the concept of lifelong learning. Whereas in the traditional educational paradigm the teacher may see his or her role as being primarily that of a transmitter of knowledge, attitudes, and skills; under the learner managed learning paradigm the role of the teacher now becomes more that of a facilitator and resource to the process of enquiry directed by the learners themselves. At least in the formative years it is the extent to which teachers are involved in facilitation that will determine the rate and extent of growth experienced by a child and, *ipso facto*, will lay the base for the difference between ten years' experience and one year's experience ten times as that child grows into adulthood and accepts responsibility for their overall development. This will be developed further in Chapter 11 where the issue of learner managed learning within the educational context will be discussed.

Both recurrent education and learner managed learning recognise that the way people learn and their learning needs – personal, familiaral, communal, and occupational – change at different stages during their lives. The difference between them is how these needs are met. Learner managed learning stresses the andragogical approach in which the individual takes responsibility for their own learning while recurrent education has a predisposition towards a pedagogical approach in which the education system is the disseminator of knowledge. (Andragogy and Pedagogy will be discussed in Chapter 4). It is true that, on page 4 of their paper, the Centre for Continuing Education argues that the apparent dichotomy between the needs of the individual and those of society are avoided through 'policies which favour a more constructive, energising, synthesis of individual learning needs with social purposes', but despite this, throughout the paper, the clear impression one obtains is that the educational system knows and provides what is best, with the individual slotting into whichever aspect is closest to the meeting of his or her needs. It is problems with our traditional educational paradigm that prompt writers such as Ross (1986) and Dalton and Thompson (1986) to question the traditional paradigm and posit approaches which are far closer to the self-directed approach which I am advocating.

The mid-career crisis

Another issue that warrants discussion at this point is that of mid-career crises. This is a relatively new concept which Hunt (1981) defines as 'a period of depression, often extending over several years, in which one has to appraise what one has achieved so far.' Hunt argues that this period is often very painful and can produce such symptoms as aggression, cynicism, hostility, alcoholism, 'pill-popping', marital breakdown, paranoia, and manic depressive behaviour. He sees physiological symptoms (usually seen to be psychosomatic) as being respiratory diseases, insomnia, malaise, headaches, cramps, back aches, etc which can produce long-term debilitating illnesses. This is the stage in which dissatisfaction with work, with one's employer, with one's career, with one's spouse and family, are also commonly reported as symptoms. It is the time at which, in the words of one of my colleagues, 'one has to decide to take Drucker's advice and divorce either one's job or one's wife.'

Hunt argues that white collar clerical and administrative positions in large, highly structured, service industries suffer the highest incidence of mid-career crisis. In analysing further variables he ascertained that age was predictive as also was lower socio-economic background and lower educational level. He found that 65 per cent of the depressed men in his sample felt that they were locked into their careers and that they were unable to change even though the majority would choose another career if they could. He found that most depressed managers believe the problems are not their fault and that they are overwhelmed by forces over which they have no control.

Hunt is not the only writer on mid-career crises. Hunt (1979 and 1981), Jaques (1965), Jung (1933), Kets de Vries (1978), Levinson, D (1976, 1978), Levinson, H (1969), Molander (1976), Pascal (1975), Rogers (1973), and Sofer (1970) are just some of the writers who refer to this issue in one form or another. Common to all of the writers is this sense of frustration that people feel because of a sense of helplessness in relation to progressing as individuals and experiencing any concept of growth or self-actualisation. Recurrent education has been tried as a means of dealing with this by suggesting people change careers or take up some new pursuit or study. In many instances such activities have proved successful but, all too often, the new training or the move to a new career results in even more frustration because, at a mature age, the person involved is competing with younger perhaps better qualified contemporaries in the new field.

I suggest that the concept of learner managed learning as the key to lifelong learning and development is a further tool available for helping people experiencing mid-career crisis. If, throughout our entire educational system, we are encouraging people to take responsibility for their own growth and development then we are providing a means of self-empowerment to individuals so that they realise much of the problem is not their situation but rather their response to it. If they perceive themselves as being powerless and dependent on other people for their growth and development then, when there is a perceived blockage in such growth and development frustration will develop and the mid-career crisis may well be the result. As will be discussed in Chapter 6, learner managed learning moves power away from people and things external to the learner over to the learner him or herself. As people gain a sense of self-empowerment the ability to deal with frustration is heightened and issues such as mid-career crisis should, I suggest, become less prevalent and traumatic.

Again this returns us to the concept of relevance in education and learning. Learner managed learning encouraging the concept of lifelong learning and development encourages an approach in which people seek out learning that is relevant to their present needs as preparation for the future. This approach challenges the concept of relevance in traditional education and, indeed, in many recurrent educational programmes. It means that we must ensure learning which enables individuals to cope with a society experiencing rapid change so that these people do not experience stagnation and/or crisis. Learner managed learning seeks to meet this issue of relevance by stressing the framework for lifelong commitment to learning. It encourages constant feedback in evaluation of experience together with goal setting, planning, and an orientation towards achievement that results in growth and development.

It is this dilemma that was faced by Barbara in the anecdote at the start of this chapter. Her emphasis had been on recurrent education and, in this regard, she had done very well. She was an achiever.

She knew where she wanted to go and she was constantly setting goals and measuring her progress towards them. Faced, however, with a changing society yet a stagnating career she challenged the relevance of her education and her career goals with the result that, because her employer was unable to facilitate her growth and learning she moved out of an excellent company and her employers lost an excellent executive.

3 The Environment for Learner Managed Learning

Case study: *Sic gloria transit*

Crichtons is a major manufacturing company with operations throughout the world. In Australia it was 50 per cent owned by the American parent and a local organisation. In the period up to 1982 the company had lost market share because of an emphasis towards preparing for the future. It had remained profitable but, rather than aggressively seeking new markets or even maintaining existing markets, it had gone through a period of people development and organisational-culture change so that the emphasis was on quality being built in to every product. In 1982 the chief executive retired and the new CEO was appointed from amongst the ranks of those who had experienced the period of people development. The emphasis now changed. Recognising that quality had become a hallmark of the company, a concentrated effort was made on expanding market share and increasing profitability. So successful was this effort that, by 1985, the Australian subsidiary had become the dominant unit within the group and the company became recognised as a leader throughout the world.

During 1987, in conjunction with my role in promoting and tutoring on Brunel University's MBA programme by extension through Henley Management College, I was discussing executive development with the new CEO and he made this comment: 'Anybody wanting to do an MBA around here is asking to resign. Our emphasis is on making and selling our products not on having managers and executives doing courses and studies.'

How self-directed is self-directed learning?

I have argued so far that learning is an active process in which individuals either seek out education and experiences or obtain feedback and do evaluation as they move through life's experiences. An essential ingredient, if this is to be a positive aspect of growth, is that the environment in which people operate must be conducive to them seeking out new learning. In theory this is the situation in most corporations and educational institutions. A regular response when I seek to discuss human resource development (HRD) in organisations is that part, at least, of the HRD concept is to foster potential in people and to encourage them to develop. The question of whether or not this is true in fact must be examined.

Knowles (1975) defines self-directed learning as:

> That process in which individuals take the initiative, with or without the help of others, in diagnosing their learning needs, formulating learning goals, identifying human and material resources for learning, choosing and implementing learning strategies, and evaluating learning outcomes.

Because there appears to be some misunderstanding of Knowles' concept as this is reflected in popular usage of the term 'self-directed learning', I am using the term 'learner managed learning' for the same concept.

Many organisations, because they conduct training needs analyses and ask the individual and organisation to identify needs, argue that they are involved in self-directed learning. In some instances they are but, in many of the organisations of which I have personal knowledge, such an approach is a means by which the organisation says 'this is the training that you are going to get'. In this instance any argument that self-directed learning is occurring becomes a veneer. The responsibility for learning is not being taken by the learner but rather an attempt is being made by the organisation to sell the learner on a decision which the organisation has made already. A key distinction in self-directed learning or, in my terms, learner managed learning, is that the learner takes responsibility for decisions as to what is being learned and the means by which learning is to take place. This will be developed further in Chapter 12. The question of who makes the decision about the learning process and topics is a key question as to whether or not learner managed learning exists. The way in which this question is answered tells us much about the environment in which any learning will take place and especially in which learner managed learning may occur.

This very question raises the issue of organisational values. In an organisation that is strongly hierarchical and in which the decision-making processes are top-down then, no matter what may be said by people within the organisation, doubt must be raised as to whether or not learner managed learning can really occur. In fact, in very many instances, I question whether learning of any sort can flourish in such an environment as all too often those attending these courses do so unwillingly and without receiving appropriate support from their supervisors and managers. Most trainers and management educators are familiar with the 'prisoner of war' syndrome in which trainees and course participants are present under duress; participate only for political reasons; and are seeking every opportunity to avoid the experience and escape from it.

I suggest that part of the reason for this is because, in Maslow's terms, we aim in training as well as in general education towards meeting what Maslow terms 'deficiency motivation needs. Maslow (1968:46f) raises the possibility that the person who is primarily meeting deficiency motivation needs will enhance the dangers of any situation and minimise the attractions. This is seen in practice. Many of the people who are involved in purported learning experiences can pay intellectual assent to what is being covered but, rather than seeking to avail themselves of these experiences and to exhibit behavioural change as a result of the programme, they respond with the assertions that they will not be able to use this in the workplace as their superiors have not attended such a programme or do not themselves utilise such approaches. Their emphasis is on protecting their own position by ensuring they do not act in such a way as would attract attention to them by their peers or superiors. Much of the money that organisations and governments spend on training and education is wasted because the environment in which such training and education is provided or should be applied is not conducive to positive growth experiences but rather is seeking to meet legislative requirements or pressures from appropriately interested groups who have a vested interest in providing programmes whether or not learning in the sense of behavioural change really occurs.

Part of the reason for this is that organisations are tempted to take short-term solutions to long-term problems. One does not need to examine many management theories or popularist approaches to organisational problems before becoming aware of this. Many extremely good management techniques ultimately receive bad publicity and are discarded because people have tried to use them in inappropriate ways. For every organisation and individual who has a positive thing to say about such issues as 'quality circles', 'just in time management', 'transactional analysis', 'grid theory', 'management by objectives' (to mention but a few) it is easy to find several others who will decry the approach as being inappropriate or less than useful.

As an illustration of this tendency to take short-term solutions to long-term problems consider the following example from a process engineering organisation:

Following a period of considerable stability and low turnover of staff throughout the organisation the machine shop area started to experience high labour turnover. Initially it was thought that this was simply a reaction after a period of low labour turnover and, accordingly, was part of a cycle relating to this issue. However, the turnover continued and was not mirrored in any other part of the organisation. Management's initial response was to ignore the problem and then, realising it would not go away, decided that it was a 'training problem' and accordingly sent the supervisor on appropriate training courses. The problem persisted the supervisor was threatened with replacement. He argued that the issue of staff selection was the problem. Accordingly the organisation re-wrote job descriptions and provided training to the supervisor and all other people involved in staff selection. The problem persisted and the decision was made to replace the supervisor. Just before action was taken to effect this dismissal a new personnel officer was appointed. He was given this problem as one requiring solution. His first action was to go down and meet the supervisor. When he got there he found that the environment was dirty and smelly. He asked as to the responsibility for cleaning and was told by the supervisor that this was part of the normal factory cleaning operations. He enquired of the factory manager and was told that this was the responsibility of the supervisor. Further discussion elicited the information that, some years before, there had been a major dispute between the then supervisor and the cleaning/maintenance staff which resulted in the supervisor saying he would be responsible for cleaning that area. That supervisor had long since left the organisation and no one had bothered to pass on that information. Accordingly preventive maintenance and cleaning had not been done – only essential crisis maintenance was occurring. Steps were taken to remedy this and the problem ceased to exist. People found that the working environment was satisfactory and did not seek to avoid it.

Far fetched? A figment of the imagination or something drawn from ancient history? No. This event actually occurred in Melbourne during the 1980s in a very well known listed public company. To me it seems incredible that in the late twentieth century, management could have failed to see such an obvious issue as lack of proper cleaning and maintenance. Yet the fact remains that this was the case and, rather than face up to their own inadequacies and seek the real solution, they sought a 'quick fix' of training. They wanted a short-term answer to a complex and long-term problem. Although this may be an extreme example, similar examples of the 'quick fix syndrome' are not isolated and virtually every organisation with which I am involved has a string of such anecdotes about short-term solutions to long-term and complex problems. In such an environment learner managed learning cannot occur and, in fact, any learning apart from that designated to meet deficiency motivation needs is unlikely to be sanctioned or utilised.

In part the concept of learner managed learning has itself been used by some people as a 'quick fix'. In such instances it is common to encounter statements as 'we leave it up to our people to determine what training they need and to organise such training'. Invariably investigation shows that such organisations spend little or no money on people development and the claim of utilising learner managed learning is provided as an excuse for inadequate training policies and practices. It also gives opportunity to blame the individual rather than the organisation when performance problems persist.

Outside of the general management area we find that there are those within the educational system who advocate learner managed learning as an easier approach in the classroom. As any teacher knows, preparation for classes is time-consuming and onerous if done properly. For this reason some educators prefer to use a standard lecture format rather than an interactive approach. They seek to develop a particular lecture or series of lectures and to deliver those year after year regardless of whether or not the information contained therein is relevant. (I was amazed when, during 1989, I encountered, in Australia, the current use of a sales case study in which all values were expressed in pounds, shillings and pence and still utilised pre-decimalisation values throughout. This after more than twenty years since decimalisation!) Educators who have this mind set seem to see themselves as the disseminators of knowledge rather than as facilitators in the learning process. I have observed a number of instances over recent years in which people with this mind set try to introduce learner managed learning as a means of avoiding their responsibility to prepare. In such instances they argue that, as the learner is responsible for his or her own learning goals and learning processes, it is the learner's fault if learning does not take place and the role of the educator is to sit back and simply to encourage the learner. Learner managed learning is not an easy option within the educational or training process. If learner managed learning is going to be used within the educational environment then it will require more, not less preparation by the facilitator so that each learner is helped individually through his or her learning process with interaction occurring on a one-to-one basis rather than on a one to large group basis. In this instance the demands on facilitators will be heightened not lessened.

Many traditional environments are hostile to learner managed learning. This hostility may not openly be expressed. Rather, in the actions and responses to those who wish to undertake learner managed learning, the hostility will become apparent. In the business/commercial sphere this hostility will be shown by such actions as making it clear that unless a particular programme is undertaken an individual's career path may be curtailed. By subtle and not so subtle means, even if nothing is stated specifically, the message will be made clear that conformity to the organisation's training plans is required if a future is desired within that organisation. In the general educational system it will be argued that the emphasis is on teaching academic and social skills that will enable individuals to fit into our society and to prepare themselves for their future occupation. The fact that such an approach pre-supposes all individuals can learn equally well by the same teaching methodology and techniques in the same educational environment is largely ignored. Failures to respond positively with the process will be blamed on the student rather than on the system itself. Persons will be referred to as 'drop-outs' rather than time being spent to ascertain what the environment is in which that person will best learn.

Self-actualisation

If learner managed learning is to become a real force then we need to change the environment in which learning takes place. Although learner managed learning will, of necessity, include some aspect of meeting deficiency motivation needs, it is apparent that for optimum functioning it must be geared towards the meeting of growth motivation needs.

Maslow coined the phrase 'self-actualisation' yet he is among the first to admit that it is not possible to define this area sharply. Growth, individuation, autonomy, self-actualisation, self-development, productiveness, self-realisation, are all crudely synonymous designating a vaguely perceived area rather than a sharply defined concept. The emphasis that Maslow seeks to make is that growth and/or self-actualisation should be seen as a process of becoming rather than a static state. Accordingly, if we are looking at introducing learner managed learning or creating an environment in which learner managed learning can flourish, we need to create a situation in which people are striving for something rather than simply seeking to meet a balance between the forces they encounter or to cope with the vagaries of everyday existence. The environment that is most conducive to learner managed learning is one in which attempt is made to build on the strengths of an individual rather than to highlight their weaknesses and to encourage that person to move beyond their current level to something more profound.

This has implications throughout our educational process. If we want an environment in which learner managed learning is encouraged then, from very earliest days we will need to reinforce positively any attempt to undertake learning. We will follow this by encouraging goal setting and learning contracts. In this regard we will assist individuals to determine appropriate areas of growth in different environments. In part this is sought by many of the alternative educational systems that have emerged in the last thirty or so years. Despite this, the vast majority of children go through an educational process that is oriented towards a passive reception of knowledge rather than an active involvement in learning.

Perhaps the changing perception of the teaching profession is partly to blame for this. Certainly within Australia there has been a down-grading of the status of teacher in the eyes of many people. Many factors have contributed towards this, including the taking of strike action by teachers with the consequent disruption to pupils and schedules. But, at least in part, such action by teachers has been a reaction to a loss in real income and a perceived degrading of conditions under which education is provided. The dismal reality today is that, in practice even if not in theory, all too often rather than being a change agent who is a partner in facilitating new ways for people to learn important skills while they gain maximum approval and reinforcement, many teachers opt for the didactic approach. There is a need for teachers to be trained in the skills that will enable them to ensure their learners embark upon a process of lifelong learning – that process in which they realise learning is not an issue which is ever completed but rather is a continuing process in which the individual is responsible for success or failure depending on the degree of commitment and involvement given.

Dalton and Thompson (1986) suggest that there are four stages through which people evolve. The first of these is a learning role or apprenticeship, the second stage is that at which a person becomes an independent contributor within their particular discipline, the third stage sees them involved in a training interface with subordinates and outside bodies, while the fourth stage is that of shaping the direction of an organisation and acting as a sponsor. These career stages are only possible if a person is experiencing growth. The failure of our educational processes, whether through the formal education system or organisational training approaches, is such that very few people really develop to the third and fourth stages while vast numbers scarcely function as an individual contributor in the second stage. This is a situation that needs attention. I suggest that the failure of so many people to develop along such a career continuum is in no small part due to the failure of early educational experiences to instil a desire for learning and a love of education. We have not provided an environment in which lifelong learning and learner managed learning is encouraged. Accordingly as Knowles (1984) says, schools have become a place in which people get hurt.

For learner managed learning to operate effectively we need to change the paradigm within which we consider the entire educational and learning process. This is not a new contention. As far back as 1931, Whitehead called for a change in our approach and, as already indicated, this call has been repeated consistently ever since. While appreciating that change can take a long time I suggest that virtually sixty years is time enough in which to move from a predominantly didactic, pedagogic approach through to the encouragement of learner managed learning and an andragogic approach – where appropriate.

The opening anecdote relating to Crichtons typifies the failure to change paradigms. It is the true and all too common example of a company experiencing considerable shifts in emphasis depending on the chief executive's orientation. An emphasis on preparing for the future through people development and culture change is not contradictory to developing market share and increasing profitability. Similarly an emphasis on expanding market share and increasing profitability does not mean that people development must be curtailed. The result of seeing these two emphases as being mutually exclusive had a predictable outcome. Within three years of this statement being made to me by the chief executive officer, Crichtons had been the victim of a take-over and the CEO to whom I had spoken was no longer employed by Crichtons or its parent.

4   Andragogy and Pedagogy

Case study: *Don't treat me like a child*

Diane is 17 years old and approaching the end of her time at high school. She has a good scholastic record and should be expected to graduate in the top 5 per cent of her class. Outside school she has a strong involvement with the scouting movement and, because of her willingness to do part-time work, she has accumulated a significant bank balance against her future university studies. She is a pleasant, easy natured girl with a stable home life and appears to be generally well adjusted.

Recently Diane's parents got a shock. There were different impressions of Diane at school from those away from school. They received a letter from the school principal expressing concern over Diane's poor academic performance in two subjects as well as her repeated absences from certain classes. Discussions with Diane provided the information that the subjects in which her standards had dropped were also the same classes that she was missing. As previously, these had been among her very best subjects. Her parents probed a little further and discovered that this year she had a new teacher. Of this teacher Diane said 'he's such a bore. He treats us as though we were still ten years old.'

Change in self-concept

In Chapter 1 reference was made to andragogy and pedagogy. Recently Knowles (1984:55f) developed some of his earlier writings on the difference between the teaching of children and the teaching of adults. He finds the term 'pedagogy for adults' to be a contradiction in terms as he points out that, by definition, pedagogy is the teaching of children. His concern is that there is a tendency to use the same style in teaching whether we are dealing with children or adults.

In Chapter 3 I called for a change in the paradigms within which we offer education and learning. The emphasis of the new paradigm advocated is to recognise the normal process of psychological growth which occurs as an individual develops from an infant to an adult.

Knowles argues that this psychological growth – whether or not reflecting psychological health – has four main areas: change in self-concept; experience; readiness to learn; and the orientation towards learning.

Any parent knows the joy (and pain) of watching their child develop a sense of identity. We are all familiar with the transition from a helpless baby who does virtually nothing apart from eat and sleep, through those early exploratory stages of discovering hands, feet, and other people, to the time when communication starts insofar as the baby becomes aware of its ability to attract attention from other people by means of smiles and sound. From my own experience of watching my children develop from this first stage of awareness through to the point of mobility and the exercise of independence it is quite clear that different approaches need to be taken with children at different stages in their development. Those involved in child psychology and education have been acknowledging this for years and the text books are full of examples and information. Despite this, time and time again, we find that young people who, at the age of two, three, four, and five enjoyed learning and trying new things have, by puberty and beyond, turned away from education and learning; have become 'problems', and are seeking opportunities to opt out of school and, all too often, their families. I suggest that this happens too frequently to ignore and yet our attempts to deal with the issue appears to do little more than exacerbate the problem.

One of the issues that it seems to me that we have difficulty with is that of the move from dependence to independence. This is true not just in the parent/child relationship but is true also in the teacher/student relationship and in the employer/employee relationship. In all areas of life we ought to have decreasing levels of dependence of one party upon another. In a totally healthy environment there is a balance between all of the bodies or systems involved. It is when one body or system dominates that we get ecological imbalance and environmental problems such as the greenhouse effect or destruction of wildlife. We need to realise that for healthy development of people a similar balance is required in which an inter-dependence develops with each party recognising a degree of dependence on the other and, as a result, experiencing a true synergy. Unfortunately it appears as though our traditional concept of dominant and subordinate units overrides this and so changes aiding this dependence – independence relationship tend to be more cosmetic than real. The result is 'problems' at home, at school, at work, and in society in general.

I am not denying the impact of family influence and peers upon this change. Nor am I entering the sociological debate of economics, class, and general discrimination. To my mind there is some aspect of class, race, sex, age, colour, and creed discrimination occurring in every country in the world. We may not like it and we may do what we can to correct it, but the fact remains that it exists. My argument for a change in paradigm is that, if we are to deal with issues such as this turn away from education and learning we need to pay attention to the causes and process over which we have some control rather than the outcome which is all too obvious. In other words, rather than placing an ambulance at the foot of the cliff, we are better to place a fence at the top.

One of the earliest drives that I have observed in children is that of the need for control. As they develop any sense of identity they wish to have some control over the things that they do. Watch the first time a child objects to being carried up or down the stairs and prefers instead to crawl up or down them. Watch, a little later, as the child starts to stand on those same stairs and then, clutching against the wall, starts to walk up the stairs. Watch the move from a child wanting the parent to put one block on another to the stage where the child starts building towers on their own. Quite apart from the personal control factors of toilet training and hygiene or even the issues of feeding and dressing themselves, in these small areas we see a movement towards some control over what is happening. It is quite clear that instinctively a child recognises the need to learn certain things in order to function effectively as an individual. As this awareness grows more and more learning occurs. The child quickly learns that behaviour such as crying and/or screaming to attract attention while having a reasonably high level of tolerance in a baby has a very low level of tolerance and acceptability by the time schooling starts. Similarly the child generally recognises a need to learn to speak, to read, to write, and to do basic calculations. At this stage it is appropriate for a predominantly pedagogical approach to be used but, even at these very early years, it is apparent that the more attractive such learning can be made by means of games, experience, simulation, and the like, the more likely it is that the child will embrace such learning and growth will occur at a relatively rapid rate.

The approach in which teachers and society primarily determine the curricula and teaching methodologies – in other words our traditional paradigm for education – becomes decreasingly relevant as this change in self-concept develops. Knowles (1984:55) argues that a point eventually occurs at which a child achieves a concept of essential self-direction and it is this point at which he sees a child becoming psychologically an adult.

Our educational and training paradigm must adapt to this change in self-concept. In a pedagogical approach the direction comes from the teacher. If we perpetuate this approach then, as the individual develops in self-concept, he or she will tend to act negatively in learning situations that are in conflict with their sense of self-identity. When this conflict occurs there is a high probability that the student will react with resistance that manifests itself either in disruptive behaviour or in compliant behaviour during the session but totally negative once the programme is concluded. It is my contention that many of the disciplinary problems encountered in schools, universities, and training sessions are directly related to this conflict between self-concept and the teaching methodology utilised. This will be discussed further in Chapter 6 when the issue of power is canvassed.

Closely related with all of this is the area of confidence. An individual who has a healthy self-concept tends to have a realistic assessment of their strengths and weaknesses. Accordingly such a person will have little difficulty in expressing themselves in relation to those things that are within their capabilities and very little reluctance to seek help in areas of deficiency. One of the strengths I have observed within much of the educational system within the U.S.A. is that the proportion of young people who exhibit high levels of confidence and self-assurance appears to be greater than in many other parts of the world. Unfortunately, rather than seeking to implement educational processes that have a higher probability of enhancing the self-concept, there is a tendency in Australia to denigrate the confident young American as being over-confident, brash, and 'cocky'. Our new paradigm must be one in which the growth towards self-confidence is encouraged even if such growth makes those of us who are older somewhat uncomfortable when our traditional ways of doing things or our comfortable mind sets are challenged.

The role of experience

Closely related to the self-concept is the role of experience. A young child has no concept of self-identity. It identifies itself totally in relation to family and people or places that are important to the family. Part of the growth towards maturity is an increasing identification of oneself in terms of ones own experiences. These experiences move from the early stages of being something that happened to a child (ie beyond the child's control) to the adult stage in which experience is who that person is (ie they are initiated or controlled by the person). When the experience of a person is denigrated in any way by being devalued or ignored then the adult is likely to perceive this as a rejection of themselves as a person.

Pedagogy does not take experience into account as much as it ought. It has the philosophy that undertaking learning is an experience to which the individual is to be subjected and that the teacher or trainer is the expert who will impart all appropriate knowledge. There is a very real sense in which a pedagogical approach argues that the only valid experience from which to move is that of the teacher. Where the experience of the teacher is significantly different from that of the members of the class then conflict is a very real possibility.

Again consider a young child. Having developed from the rolling over stage to the process of crawling, eventually the child starts to stand and, in the course of time, starts to walk. In the early stages of walking there will be many instances in which the child reverts to crawling because experience has indicated that, by crawling, they can get from point A to point B reasonably easily. As confidence grows in walking the time comes when crawling is seldom used. Rather, experience has taught the child that by walking from point A to point B he or she will cover the distance more rapidly and with less wear and tear on the knees. At such a stage any attempt to get the child to revert to crawling will be seen as a game of which one quickly tires because that which is being taught or performed is different to what experience has shown is the most satisfactory way of travelling.

Similar situations are seen when one moves between various national cultures. My teaching experience with both undergraduate and graduate students in countries as diverse as New Zealand, Australia, Great Britain, Singapore, and the U.S.A. has convinced me of the need to ascertain something of the background and general experience of my students prior to embarking upon my teaching duties. Even within such a country as the United States there tend to be tremendous differences of experience between undergraduate students in Philadelphia, graduate students in Cincinnati, and both undergraduate and graduate students in Los Angeles. A failure to recognise these differences and to adapt ones approach can result in a disastrous experience for both learners and teacher. This will be examined a little more in Chapter 13.

The andragogic approach seeks to use the experience of learners as a resource in the entire learning process. In this regard the teacher takes time to relate to each learner as an individual and, by so doing, places a high value on the experience of individuals and, *ipso facto*, thus implies a high value for the individual himself or herself. From this base the teaching approach used is adapted so as to move from the known to the unknown in a way that is most appropriate for the rate and style of assimilation of knowledge of that person. Accordingly, by such an approach learners are encouraged to evaluate experience and to use that as a launching pad for growth.

Readiness to learn

Somewhere between early childhood and adolescence there is, for far too many people, a dramatic drop in the orientation towards learning. There can be few things that are more exciting than watching a child explore its surroundings, experiment with whatever is to hand, and learn. Watching a child recognise objects, eventually come to speak of those objects, and, ultimately, to make the transition from concrete experience to abstract thought can be very humbling. When very young, learning is part of the adventure of life; by adolescence far too many children find it a chore to be avoided.

It is true that there are different degrees of readiness to learn at different stages in our overall development but surely part of the responsibility of any person involved in the educational process is to seek to heighten the readiness to learn rather than to stifle it.

Certainly there are different things that must be learnt at different stages in our personal development. As a young child we need to learn that behaviour which is socially acceptable as opposed to that which is not socially acceptable. In our early schooling we need to learn to read, write, and do arithmetic. In our working situations we need to learn the skills that will enable us to function effectively. These are appropriate issues to be taught in conjunction with the developmental process. The trap that we must avoid is to treat every person as though they were developing at the same rate and so take a standardised approach. While, statistically, we can be assured that such a standardised approach will meet the needs of the vast majority of any population we can be equally sure that it will create difficulties for many as there will not be an appropriate match between readiness to learn and that which is being taught. The andragogical approach assumes that there are certain things an adult must know in order to function effectively at different stages of development. Accordingly the needs of education and training will differ according to the experience and stage of development of the trainee. In this concept the learner has a large amount of input as to what is taught and when it is taught. If this can be extended so that attention is paid to the readiness to learn from earliest days then we will find that, rather than being turned off from education and learning there will be a continuing readiness to undergo the learning experience.

Orientation of learning

The readiness to learn that is shown by an individual is, in effect, their orientation towards learning. There are two sides to this orientation. The first is that of the learner and the second is that of the teacher, trainer, or professor. In order to discuss comprehensively the principles of adult learning we need to consider the orientation of the people providing the learning experiences. It is this that is referred to as the orientation of learning.

Pedagogy bases itself on a subject oriented approach to learning. In this situation there are certain subjects that must be taught and in which the learner must gain competence. Accordingly results are achieved in relation to subjects studied and either passed or failed. For virtually every person to whom I speak their key educational experiences have been obtained within such a framework.

Obviously such an approach is appropriate in early formal learning experiences and in some subject areas. It is futile to seek involvement and participation from any person until they know enough about the subject or task in order to know even what questions to ask. For this reason there is a sense in which some form of a pedagogic approach is necessary in most educational training situations.

Andragogy extends this. Andragogy is a problem-centred education. Because andragogy is geared to particular developmental cycles through which the individual is passing then, what is being sought are solutions to problems currently being faced or about to be faced. Often the person may not look for answers to such problems but rather a way of confronting and dealing with them. In other words they are looking not for content but for process.

What this means is that the andragogic approach deals with the whole concept of learning not from the point of view that says 'certain subjects must be passed' but from the perspective of saying 'there are certain problems or issues that must be dealt with'.

Again relate this to life experience. Early mathematics in terms of adding, subtracting, multiplying, and dividing are generally seen as being relatively related to life because every child knows that necessities of life must be purchased and they are quickly accustomed to paying for goods and receiving change. Consequently although general arithmetic may be seen as a little bit tedious it is recognised as being essential for effective functioning. This is not so true when it comes to more advanced subjects such as algebra, geometry, trigonometry, and calculus. If these are taught in a purely abstract way or by the rote learning of formulae and the solving of classroom exercises then disinterest can quickly arise. Most people who have trouble with mathematics experience such difficulties not because they are unable to deal with mathematical concepts but because the way they have been taught the subject has shown them no direct link between theoretical mathematics and practical life.

As an illustration of this consider a class of 15 year olds in high school for whom subjects such as mathematics and physics were important only because high passes in these subjects when applying for university would enable them to enter the courses of their choice. Their ability to apply the mathematical principles to everyday life was low even though they knew the formulae and could work classroom exercises. Into this class came a teacher for whom mathematics was a thrilling subject with high relevance to everyday living. Within three months he had transformed the class from one which was attended through a sense of duty to one which was eagerly anticipated and instilled in those boys a lifelong regard for the beauty of mathematics and an enduring belief that they had relevance in every area of life. The difference between Terry and previous teachers was that Terry started from concrete experience. He introduced us to engineers who were involved in road and bridge building; he arranged for us to calculate the stresses and strains that would be encountered in the building of a major road through a heavily populated part of the city; and he arranged for the engineers to review with us our figures and the relevance of our designs. Terry changed our paradigm. We were used to the pedagogical approach and Terry moved it into a problem centred, process oriented investigation of real life issues that enabled us to solve real life problems. Some thirty years later when I meet fellow members of that class we find that there is a common awareness of our indebtedness to Terry and his style of teaching for our future careers and, for those of us who are involved in teaching, for the approach we take in the classroom situation.

What andragogy is all about is applied knowledge. What learner managed learning is all about is encouraging us to seek out the knowledge that we need as we progress through life and to open our minds to the potential of formal and informal learning occurring from every experience.

The argument being assembled is not one which says we must dispose of pedagogy. Rather the argument being assembled is saying that we must examine where pedagogy is appropriate and recognise that, as an individual grows and develops, there is a need for a shift in paradigm away from a pedagogical approach through to an andragogical approach. It is only by making this transition that we will be encouraged to embrace the concept of life long learning and see the relevance of self-direction in the entire learning process.

This is the problem faced by Diane. The normal growth processes of life were encouraging her to learn in ways other than 'being taught'. She felt the need for an andragogic approach and, instead, continued to experience pedagogy. Was it any wonder she 'turned off'?

5 Experiential Learning and Learner Managed Learning

Case study: *Building blocks and light bulbs*

Norman was having an interesting discussion. He was meeting with the head of a tertiary institution and they were discussing problems encountered with teaching methodologies. The more Norman listened the more it seemed to him that the academic staff were divided into two camps. On the one hand were those who believed all education had to be provided in a step-by-step fashion, building block upon block until a comprehensive covering of the subject or topic was completed. On the other hand were those who sought to take an experiential approach but, from time to time, failed to process the experiment adequately. These people seemed to expect that, as a result of an exercise or experience, there would be the sudden turning on of a light bulb in the mind of the learner so that they could make the transition from the concrete experience to the application of that experience both in terms of general theory and also in application.

It seemed to Norman that, rather than an either/or situation, the two approaches were complementary.

What is experiential learning?

So far I have considered the overall concept of learning and have compared lifelong learning with recurrent education. Another concept which needs to be explored in these early chapters is that of experiential learning. Experiential learning is that learning experience which arises from first of all undergoing a particular experience then, as a result of reflecting upon that experience, extrapolating learning from it.

During the last twenty or so years there has been a significant increase in material relating to experiential learning. As a result of this, most trainers, teachers and professors today use some aspects of experiential learning.

Experiential learning is a method involving a reasonable degree of risk. It assumes that the trainer, teacher, or professor is able to operate as a facilitator in the learning process and that, if the experience goes other than planned, he or she will be able to cope with changes in the envisaged situation. This means that, if experiential learning is to be used, the facilitator needs extensive training in the process and must be completely familiar with all aspects of the material being used.

Most of the material available on experiential learning suggests that there are five steps involved. They are:

1. Experiencing.
2. Publishing.
3. Processing.
4. Generalising.
5. Applying.

Experiencing

Central to the concept of experiential learning is the premise that participants on a programme come from a variety of backgrounds. Even if their backgrounds are similar there are still differences in their overall life experience. Accordingly the intention is to have these people share a common experience so that there is some particular point at which their various backgrounds merge. Ideally this shared activity helps participants to understand more of themselves as well as of other people within the group.

I believe that, ideally, these experiences should be positive and designed in such a way as to provide a low level of personal risk for every participant.

Publishing

Once the experience is completed then the publishing phase is that at which participants share their opinions of what has occurred and their perceptions of the results obtained. The emphasis here is not on understanding the experience but simply obtaining data as to what participants perceived as occurring and their reactions to this.

Processing

At this stage participants are encouraged to look beyond the experience itself to why the experience was used and what are the implications of the experience for them both individually and as a group. Generally, but not always, it is this part of the experiential learning process that will occupy the largest percentage of time available. Obviously, also at this stage, the role of the facilitator is crucial as, depending on the skill of facilitation, the processing may be shallow or profound.

Generalising

At this point the group is encouraged to move from the specific to the general. Having undergone a particular experience and shared their perceptions of it together with the implications of this, they are now encouraged to consider how this has relevance in their wider world and experience. So, at this stage, an experiential exercise relating to an accounting function having gone through the publishing phase in which participants share their observations as to the amount of knowledge they have in accounting and, from there, moved to consider the general accounting principles involved, would discuss how these principles have relevance in an everyday work situation. An exercise designed around valuation of inventory may elicit the data that various techniques are used by each participant or group in the exercise and processing may bring about an understanding of the need for the general accounting principle of inventory being valued at the lowest of cost or valuation. In the generalising phase participants will consider the valuation method used at their place of business and the implications of this for either a first in first out, a last in first out, or some other method of inventory control.

Applying

This final stage is the one at which participants move from the exercise itself to determining how the principles drawn out of the exercise are to be applied in their general life situations. This is the point at which learning leads to an action plan for implementation of the learning or, at very least, to the development of recommendations for implementing the principles deduced.

How much input?

Experiential learning is discussed by a variety of writers including Kolb, Rubin and McIntyre (1984), Newstrom and Scannell (1980, 1983), Pfeiffer and Jones (1968 and annually from then), Rackham and Morgan (1977), and Roskin (1984), to mention but a few. All writers on the subject stress that to conduct any programme using experiential learning requires significantly more preparation by the facilitator than does normal lecturing.

Experiential learning does not mean that there is no input to the learners. What it does mean is that such input takes account of the experience of each learner and seeks to build upon that experience rather than being divorced from the reality experienced by the learner. It seeks to build a bridge between general truths/principles and the specific reality of the learner. It is directly related to the 'problem-centred' concept of andragogy.

Wolf and Kolb (1984) argue that experiential learning theory provides a model of learning and adaptation processes consistent with the structure of human cognition and the stages of human growth and development. They see it as conceptualising the learning process in such a way that differences in individual learning styles and corresponding learning environments can be identified. This will be referred to further in Chapter 10. They advocate experiential learning because:

> In addition to providing a framework for conceptualising individual differences in style of adaption to the world, the experiential learning model suggests more normative directions for human growth and development. . . . Individual learning styles affect how people learn, not only in the limited educational sense, but also in the broader aspects of adaptation to life, such as decision-making, problem-solving and a lifestyle in general. Experiential learning is not a molecular educational concept, but a molar concept describing the central process of human adaptation to the social and physical environment. It, like Jungian theory, is a holistic concept that seeks to describe the emergence of basic life orientations as a function of dialectic tensions between basic modes of relating to the world. As such, it encompasses other more limited adaptive concepts, such as creativity, problem-solving, decision-making, and attitude change, that focus heavily on one or another of the basic aspects of adaptation.

The diagram shown at Figs 1 and 2 is a reproduction of Wolf and Kolb's graphic illustration of the experiential model for growth and development.

Wolf and Kolb see the four dimensions of growth as depicted by the shape of a cone in which the base represents the lowest stages of development and the apex represents the peak of development. By this they represent the fact that all four dimensions become more highly integrated at higher stages of development. In their discussion of this concept they point out that the actual process of growth in any single individual life history tends to proceed through successive oscillations from one stage to another rather than being a straight line growth process through a simple three layer cone.

Experiential learning in practice

One of the most complex studies on experiential learning is that

Figure 1   *The experiential learning theory of growth and development*

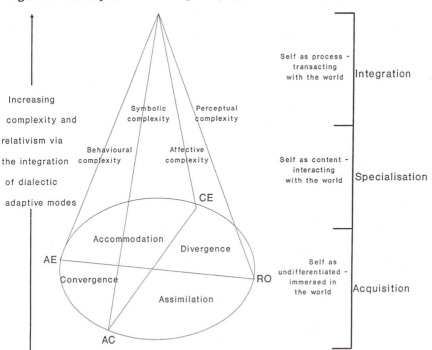

Source: Adapted from David A. Kolb, Irwin M. Rubin, James M. McIntyre, *Organizational Psychology: Readings on Human Behavior in Organizations* Fourth Edition, 1984, Prentice Hall, Inc, Englewood Cliffs, New Jersey 07632, Page 134. Used with permission.

reported by Rackham and Morgan (1977). In this report of a four year research project at British Overseas Airways Corporation (now British Airways) they set out an approach that, since then, has formed a basis for many programmes. The issue that Rackham and Morgan faced was how to improve the overall performance of an organisation by influencing the skills that employees at all levels had in dealing with others – their interactive skills. A secondary concern was the fact that many people are inept at interacting with others while most of the remainder still have a lot of room for improvement. Accordingly any programme that would have benefit for the organisation would have ongoing benefit also for individuals in their private lives. Rackham and Morgan sought to use the principles of andragogy and their book is a cross between a research report and a training manual, moving from the specific experience at BOAC through additional and later experiences to the point of generalisation. It provides valuable

Figure 2 *Comparison of the experiential learning model and the problem-solving process (modified)*

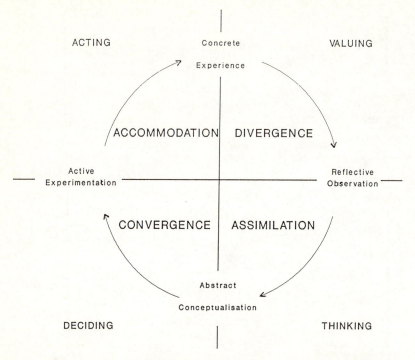

Source: Adapted from David A. Kolb, Irwin M. Rubin, James M. McIntyre, *Organizational Psychology: An Experiential Approach to Organizational Behavior*, Fourth Edition, 1984, Prentice Hall, Inc, Englewood Cliffs, New Jersey 07632, Page 40. Used with permission.

guidelines for those interested in utilising experiential learning. It provides a very clear illustration of the movement through Kolb and Fry's cone as shown earlier. Not only was the programme devised by Rackham and his team one which provided growth for the participants on the programme but it provided also significant growth in each of the facilitators. The very clear evidence throughout is that, properly used, experiential learning is an essential part of andragogy as well as promoting innovative learning.

All of this creates considerable difficulty for the individual or organisation that is locked into a traditional concept of education. With an holistic approach it is essential that individuals are able to see clearly how whatever learning is undertaken fits into the way in which they relate to their world. It brings us to examine the concept of andragogy (Chapter 4) in which learning becomes a problem-centred event that takes account of the experience of the learner and the goals which the learner has set. Experiential learning places the responsibility for the learning process jointly upon the learner and the facilitator. On the facilitator's shoulders rests the responsibility for ensuring the experiential activity becomes part of the learning process. While on the shoulders of the learner rests the responsibility for ensuring that learning goals are furthered through the experience.

To some extent it is the concept of experiential learning that can cause many of the difficulties people have with learner managed learning. Yuill (1980) discusses the impact which uncertainty as to results can have upon an organisation with centralised authority. He shows that, where uncertainty exists in such an organisation, considerable resistance can be expected by those introducing the uncertainty. As we will see (Chapters 6, 9, and 11) in the traditional training and educational paradigm (ie primarily pedagogical) such uncertainty cannot be tolerated. In the traditional scientific method, we use the approach of formulating an hypothesis, testing the hypothesis by experimentation, and then, depending on the results, either confirming the hypothesis or formulating a new hypothesis. This new hypothesis then becomes subject to further testing and the cycle is repeated. It seems as though we are not really willing to apply this extensively in the field of learning. Our hypothesis appears to have been that the pedagogical approach should be the primary format. Experience has shown that, in a very large number of instances, the pedagogical approach does not work. At the same time we have discovered that the experiential approach (based on the principles of andragogy) does work. We have found that, where there is a shared experience in which people can neither deny nor can they intellectualise the behaviours exhibited, significant steps in learning do occur. Despite that we have, in many traditional disciplines, failed to implement this.

As an illustration of this consider my experience while working with one of Australia's major training organisations. In 1985, when I joined this organisation, I examined the training techniques used in existing public programmes by means of reading both participants' material and trainers' manuals, sitting in on training programmes, and discussion with participants and trainers. I found that the vast majority of trainers were using a primarily lecture-style approach with exercises designed to reinforce what the lecturer was teaching. Generally there was no effort made to ascertain the prior knowledge or experience of participants and, in many instances, participants felt that they were being 'talked down to' by the trainer. There was no doubt that, in the vast majority of cases, both the material provided together with the knowledge and experience of the trainer was excellent. The difficulty lay in the way in which this was being presented. Accordingly I organised a series of workshops looking at the way in which experiential learning could be introduced and providing experience in participating on experiential learning programmes. These met with mixed response partly because, initially, there was a reluctance to change existing patterns of behaviour but also because the organisation itself gave no encouragement or reinforcement to the trainers for changing their approach. Both the organisation and many of the trainers tended to stress centralised authority and, as predicted by Yuill, the uncertainty of experiential learning ran into barriers because of the threat it provides to such a centralised authoritarian concept. However, in the instances where people did move to experiential learning then there was unanimous agreement that learning was helped rather than hindered by working from a common experience and following through the general pattern set out at the start of this chapter.

Experiential learning is not a panacea for any educational or learning malaise. It is not appropriate in every form of education or training and such experiences as Smart's (Chapter 13) are a remainder that the use of experiential learning must be relevant to the culture and environment of the learners. But, properly implemented, it can be an effective implementation of the principles of andragogy and a very positive step forward in the development of a learner managed learning process. If a person is serious about implementing learner managed learning and encouraging people to participate in lifelong learning experiences then understanding of and use of experiential learning activities will prove to be a valuable adjunct in the process.

Koestler (1975) discusses the either/or concept which has developed in psychology. As mentioned in Chapter 2, he discusses what he calls 'the philosophy of ratomorphism' and the difficulties of generalising on behaviour of humans and higher animals from observed behaviour in rats and pigeons. He examines the complexities of the way in which animals at all levels process information, create things, and respond to the various stimuli encountered. His contention is that there is a place for positive reinforcement and learning in a step by step fashion. There is a place also, he argues, for light bulbs to flash on as a result of experiential learning. All people learn in complex ways and the advocating of one way to the exclusion of any other produces an imbalance and creates problems. It is as Martin Luther said in one of his post-Wittenburg writings 'anything taken to extreme becomes a heresy'.

Wolf and Kolb in the model shown earlier seek to bring about a synthesis between various ways in which people learn. It is their contention (as will be discussed further in Chapter 8) that people have a predisposition towards a particular style of learning but that no person is confined to learning only by one approach, nor should trainers, professors, and teachers seek to advocate any one approach to the learning process to the total exclusion of any other. Learner managed learning enables learners to move between the various approaches available and to ensure that the appropriate synthesis is obtained that suits the individual.

Norman went on to discuss this issue with the principal to whom he was talking. They spent some time examining models for integrating learning processes. The principal agreed with Norman that an integrated approach was desirable and that the dichotomy between the two factions was really false. Despite this he felt that, under the existing approach taken by his institution and faculty, the ability to deal with this issue and to improve the situation was seriously impaired.

6 Learner Managed Learning and Power

Case study: *Push or pull?*

At fifty Graham is the youngest chief executive within a particular major multinational group. He is responsible for the Australasian operations whose turnover is in excess of $500 million per annum; almost 2,000 people are employed by the company in Australia.

Graham is a fast track person. He joined the company on leaving university and was quickly singled out as someone with potential. In his first twenty years with the company he was given increasing responsibility and gained experience working in five different countries. For the three years immediately preceding his appointment as CEO in Australia, he was personal assistant to the group chairman based in London. On the retirement of the previous Australian chief executive officer during 1988, Graham returned to his homeland as Australian managing director. Early in 1989 he was appointed chairman of the Australian operations and appointed to the board of the group holding company.

Graham has always had a strong belief in developing people's potential. He sees human resource development as being a line management function and is determined to change the culture of the Australian company so as to encourage learner managed learning and the acceptance of responsibility for people development by corporate and line management.

Soon after his appointment as chief executive officer in 1988 Graham approached me to discuss ways of changing the organisational culture and creating an environment in which learner managed learning could occur.

Graham explained that, although he had the authority to order change, he felt that it was important for him to facilitate change rather than command it. We considered various strategies and, within a few weeks, I was approached by the financial controller with the request that I conduct a half-day workshop on leadership at his next department conference. This workshop led to two further one-day workshops at subsequent conferences and, at the start of 1989, it led to a three-day residential workshop for this department. During the seven months over which these workshops occurred the controller noticed a significant reduction in labour turnover amongst his people and an improved relationship between the controller's department and the rest of the company. Where, prior to the workshops, the fourth greatest lie within this company was seen as the statement 'I'm from the controller's department and I'm here to help you' the attitude of user departments had changed to the point of actively seeking out assistance from the controller's department and a willingness to supply the controller's department with information sought.

By mid-1989 other departments were commenting on the change that had occurred in the controller's department. At this point Graham decided it was appropriate to schedule a five-day residential workshop for the board and divisional general managers (a total of 22 people) and this was scheduled for November. The first two days of the workshop were spent looking at internal issues such as corporate vision and strategies. The middle of the workshop involved input from myself and two other consultants and the final stage of the workshop was spent in developing action plans for the 90s. One of the action plans related to the implementation of learner managed learning throughout the organisation.

Power and the change in paradigm

Rogers (1973) defines power as 'potential for influence'.

One of the key emphases of my argument so far is that, for learner managed learning to become extant, there needs to be a shift in paradigm. In Chapter 4, I introduced the concept of power and stated that it would be discussed in more detail in Chapter 6. Although not always considered in books relating to learning *per se*, the issue of power is an important one in any discussion of the learning process and it becomes even more important when we are considering a change in paradigm.

Yuill (1980) argues that in an organisation with centralised structure but where there is uncertainty as to power bases and outcomes, a highly competitive situation can occur which, in extreme versions, can result in a power struggle that is totally disfunctional to the organisation. Such a situation, if continued for too long, results in the viability of the organisation becoming precarious. In this case there is a temptation to revert to the status quo so that stability can return. An example of this is provided in Chapter 10 where I discuss an organisation in which they had three chief executive officers within a two-year period. The problem with this approach is that, ultimately, it can bring about atrophy in the organisation and eventually cause the organisation's demise. Some would argue that this is already the case with many of our educational and commercial institutions.

We must note, however, that there is an equally serious danger if one simply seeks to introduce the new. Around 210 BC Petronius is purported to have said:

> We trained hard – but it seemed that every time we formed up into teams we would be reorganised . . .
>
> I was to learn later in life that we tend to meet any new situation by reorganising; and a wonderful method it can be for creating the illusion of progress while producing confusion, inefficiency, and demoralisation

In advocating learner managed learning I am not proposing that the traditional paradigm be changed simply for the sake of change. I believe that there are very sound reasons for a change to learner managed learning and these include both commercial reasons and educational ones.

Based on my experience of more than twenty years in line management, human resource development, and consulting it is my belief that at least 50 per cent of every dollar spent on training is wasted. To my mind wastage occurs whenever there is no observable behavioural change as a result of a training programme. If the programme is designed to provide knowledge then it should be measurable as to whether or not the increase in knowledge enables a person to function more effectively. If the training is to provide skills then there should be observable improvement in the quality and/or quantity of output. Such changes cannot be assumed from the report sheets at the end of a programme and, in the main, will need to be measured over a protracted period. One of the reasons why the Center for Leadership Studies introduced a three year evaluation programme for all persons undergoing training through our organisation was to obtain valid data as to whether or not we were providing value for money. Although, at the time of writing, the first such three year evaluation programme is not yet completed, the early evidence indicates that there is a significantly greater degree of observable behavioural change amongst people who are involved in a learner managed learning process than those who are attending programmes under the traditional paradigm.

The second reason for change of paradigm is an educational one. Chapter 4 discussed the relationship between andragogy and pedagogy. If we are serious about adult education then, I believe, we must be serious about learner managed learning. To my mind it is only by implementing learner managed learning that the principles of andragogy can be fully applied. This will be discussed further in Chapter 8 when I provide a model for learner managed learning.

The introduction of learner managed learning involves human interactions in all areas of an organisation – superior/subordinate, peer/peer, subordinate/superior. It is impossible to consider any human interactions without considering the concept of power. French, Raven and Cartwright (1959; 150–167) identify the sources of power as being reward power, coercive power, legitimate power, expert power, and referent power. Etzione (1961:66f) argues that organisational power is best represented as coercive, utilitarian, and normative. McLelland (1970) discusses the neutrality of power while Hersey and Blanchard

(1988:202f) argue that power is basically either personal or positional. Obviously these are but a few of the many writers on the issue of power but they serve to illustrate three key issues relating to power:

1. Power is given to an individual either by the organisation in which he or she operates or by the people with whom he or she interacts – ie The source of power.
2. Power in itself is neutral and can be either used or abused – ie The neutrality of power.
3. Both sources of power are interrelated and they are expressed in a variety of ways – ie Different expressions of power.

In order to discuss these issues it is necessary first to define what is meant by positional power and personal power. Hersey and Blanchard (1988) describe positional power as being that which enables a person to induce others to do a certain job because of the position this person has in the organisation. Accordingly positional power is the right to use rewards and sanctions in order to obtain compliance or to achieve results. Personal power, however, is derived from the people with whom one works or interacts. Accordingly personal power is the extent to which others respect, feel good about, and are committed to the person seeking to influence them.

The source of power

The traditional, pedagogic approach to learning sees the teacher as utilising positional power. In Hersey and Blanchard's concept they have power vested in them by the educational authorities and/or the organisation with which they are associated. Because of this positional power they receive a large degree of personal power from either those who entrust people into their teaching care or who come to them for learning. In terms of French and Raven they have reward power because they are able to determine whether or not a person has passed a particular course or programme; they have coercive power because they can put in an adverse report to parents or managers; they have legitimate power because they are lawfully entitled to exert influence in the learning situation; they have expert power because of the belief that they have some relevant expertise or special knowledge that their learners do not have; and they have referent power because of the modelling that they are able to do for their trainees. In Etzione's concepts they have coercive power because they are able to force their students to follow specific courses of action – the teacher or trainer devises the curriculum and the learning strategy with the learners being required to comply if they are to complete the programme satisfactorily. They have utilitarian power insofar as they can reward learners by passing or failing at the end of a test or programme; and they have normative power because most learners experience significant social pressure to be part of the learning community in which they find themselves. As McLelland points out, none of these are inherently good or bad. Accordingly, a teacher or trainer can abuse these sorts of power and can emphasise one to the detriment of others or, indeed, build up each of them to the point where it is difficult, if not impossible, to challenge the power base. Leach and Raybould (1977:2) refer to this when they argue that ordinary schools have tended to take the negative role of law enforcer and moral judge when dealing with behavioural difficulties. As I have already argued in several places, these traditional educational systems have, all too often, resulted in people being turned off from learning rather than encouraged in the concept of lifelong personal development.

Learner managed learning recognises these power bases but moves the power potential from the facilitator to the learner. In learner managed learning, learners take responsibility for their learning experience and learning goals right from the outset of the programme. This is a very threatening concept to people who have an entrenched viewpoint or mind-set in which they are the disseminators of knowledge and have the authority to control the destiny of their learners.

In an historical concept this was, *inter alia*, a cause for the Protestant reformation of the 16th century. Over the first fifteen hundred or so years since the advent of Christianity the Roman Catholic Church had come to see itself as the guardian of the faith and as having within itself the power to determine whether an individual would go to heaven or hell after death. In a world where education was the exception rather than the rule and in which few people could read or write, the ability to read the scriptures and to interpret them for the masses was an important positional power base incorporating the ability to use reward power or coercive power almost at the whim of the priest.

With the Renaissance and the rise of national languages in a written form, education became more readily available and a direct consequence of this was a desire for reading material. The advent of the printing press made possible relatively inexpensive copies of written material and at least part of the resistance encountered by such people as Wycliffe, Cramer, Tyndall, Knox, Luther, Calvin, and the other prominent reformation names, was because of the threat they provided to the traditional paradigm. Under such circumstances and against such power the surprising thing is not that opposition occurred but rather that a new paradigm ultimately became accepted to the extent that, today, virtually every Christian denomination and sect accepts the necessity for the Christian scriptures to be available in the local languages and dialects of all people.

The shift to learner managed learning has not met with a vehement opposition but it is some indication of the power bases used by those adhering to the traditional paradigm that it is more than sixty years since Alfred North Whitehead first challenged the traditional educational approaches. The most popular power base I observe today is still that of positional power and as long as our teaching and training paradigm continues to be dominated by this source of power we will experience considerable difficulty in implementing learner managed learning.

The neutrality of power

It is important to stress that I am not advocating a total move away from positional power. As McLelland says 'power is neutral – it has two faces'. My concern is that we should use positional power in a positive way. In Chapter 8 I will be developing the learner managed learning model and, in this, I will argue that both personal and positional power have their place in the learning process. Where a person has little or no knowledge or ability in a subject or skill then, obviously, it is appropriate to use a didactic approach and, equally, it is appropriate to use rewards to reinforce learning. At times we may need to use coercion or punishment if there is a repeated failure to learn. The danger comes when we use these power bases exclusively and create a situation in which performance is only obtained when extrinsic rewards are offered or, alternatively, when performance is designed to avoid punishment rather than to achieve results. Perhaps much of the widespread agnosticism and antipathy towards traditional religions that we encounter in the late 20th century has its source in the extensive abuse of positional power that has been exhibited by virtually all religions over the past several thousand years.

Personal power has as its source the trust, respect, and esteem that is given to one person by another or others. An example of this is provided in Chapter 4 when I talk of my own high school experience with 'Terry' as my teacher. Terry certainly used positional power. There was never any doubt as to who was ultimately in charge in the classroom but the performance he obtained from our class was significantly greater than that obtained by any previous mathematics master because Terry sought to develop his personal power. He treated us as responsible adults; he listened to us; and he related our classroom situations to the real world. Certainly he used an extremely didactic approach when it was appropriate but, in addition, he was prepared to share with us in the learning experience; to admit when he did not know the answer to a question or problem; and readily to give of his own free time to assist us in our learning process. Terry had learnt the skill of using both positional and personal power in a positive way.

In our educational and training approaches we must learn the positive use of power. In order to do this we must introduce the concept of power as something which every learner has available to him or her and we must provide a format by which this learner determines the experiences to be undergone and the specific goals to be attained. This creates considerable difficulty for many trainers and facilitators whose orientation is towards a teacher or trainer centred learning experience but, if we are to develop our skills in the positive use of power then this is required. If we are to do this we must understand what power is and we must obtain a working definition of power.

There is no doubt that there is considerable confusion over the definition of power. As already stated, Rogers (1973:1418–1433) discusses power as 'the potential for influence'. It is this concept of power that I am using.

When we consider this potential for influence then we need to remember two other key things relating to it. First, power is finite. Whether we are talking about positional power or personal power there is only a specific amount that each of us has. Sooner or later, we run the risk of reaching the bounds of our power. If we use power in a negative way – ie abuse this influence potential, then we are likely to reach the bounds of our power significantly sooner than if we use it in a positive way.

The second thing is that, as the behavioural sciences have been teaching for many years, people react not to reality but to their perception of reality. In other words it is not the actual amount of power that we have but the amount of power we are perceived to have that determines our influence potential. One of the things that can lead to corruption by people in authority is that they are perceived to have more power than is actually the case and, where they decide to abuse this perception, corruption occurs. Virtually every country in the world experiences this at some time or another in areas such as politics, business, policing, public service, and the military. Either the individuals involved have a greater perception of their own power and tend to abuse it or other people have a greater perception of their power and then encourage power abuse.

In the traditional educational and training system we have to counter the experience of the negative use of power that has been used by too many educators and trainers for so long. I believe that we can do this best by fostering the concept of learner managed learning and helping in the transition of the perception of power away from the teacher or facilitator to the learner.

Different expressions of power

Botkin, Elmadjra and Malitza (1979:52) argue that concentrated power and its misuse are today the greatest obstacles to learning for survival and dignity. They suggest that power is at once the primary cause of and a potential aid in dealing with what they call 'the human gap'. They see this gap as being the difference between where we are and where we ought to be. In their argument, the dimensions of the gap may be said to reflect the incongruity between power and wisdom, and between the unimaginable potential of contemporary society for creative action and the lack of political will that fosters paralysis and inaction. They ask why today's educational systems which are larger and more advanced than at any other time in history have largely failed to respond to the challenge of global issues and so contributed to our lack of preparedness to live harmoniously in an interdependent world.

I suggest that we do not need to look far for the answer to this question. Existing educational and political organisations have a vested interest in maintaining the status quo. Traditional educational paradigms have relied primarily on positional power in all aspects of imparting knowledge. The teacher has been seen as having a very special status in the community. As I have said already it is not purely coincidental that, in most early societies, the role of teaching was closely intertwined with the role of the priesthood. In our western culture a trend away from this intertwining occurred only as recently as the Renaissance and the Reformation. In many oriental cultures the teacher continues to be seen in this elevated position – a fact which can create difficulties for the introduction of learner managed learning in such societies. (This issue will be discussed further in Chapter 13).

Inherent in this positional power concept of teaching is an implication that education is to be endured passively by the student with questions or other behaviour which could be considered to challenge the authority of the teacher or the sources referred to by the teacher, being actively discouraged and, all too often, heavily punished. It is no wonder, under this paradigm, that the concept of learner managed learning and the growth towards psychological maturity in which individuals take responsibility for their own learning has been less than enthusiastically received and acted upon.

We find expressions of positional power bases in the following selection of statements from the President of the Federation of

Australian University Staff Associations, the Chairman of the Australian Vice Chancellor's Committee, the General Secretary of the Federation of College Academics, representatives of the Federal Department of Education, and the Federal Education Minister who, in 1986, when discussing the introduction of the first private university to Australia said:

> The proposal will debase academic standards,
> The notion of a higher education institution established for profit is completely unacceptable.
> The pursuit of profit is not consistent with providing quality higher education, and
> A private university will face difficulty in having its degrees recognised in the light of government policy.

On another level we find many teachers currently decrying the absence of corporal punishment from schools and, in at least one situation personally known to me, a teacher walking out on the class and refusing to go back to the school because the class did not accord him the respect and obedience that he believed was inherent in his position as a teacher.

Each of these instances provides an example of a manifestation of the traditional paradigm which is based on positional power and which, all too often, allows itself to be abused rather than used positively.

Power has always been a reality in the educational and learning process, but often this has been forgotten or misunderstood. Any attempt to ignore its reality is an exercise in futility. If we are to bring about a change in paradigm so that lifelong learning is encouraged through the process of learner managed learning then we must learn to accept the reality of these power bases and develop the skills and the maturity to use them positively rather than seeing any change in paradigm as a serious threat to the status quo and thus a challenge to all that we hold dear.

Graham recognised the reality of power. Had he introduced the learner managed learning concept by means of a presidential edict he would certainly have got lip-service to the concept but, in the long-term, it is extremely unlikely that any significant cultural shift would have occurred in his organisation. By developing personal power and encouraging the development of personal power in the controller's department he created an environment in which opposition to the change in paradigm was minimised and, in the long-term, will ensure that learner managed learning becomes the dominant paradigm within his organisation.

7 Learner Managed Learning and Motivation

Case study: *I can and I will!*

Today Ian is a successful businessman. It was not always thus.

While at high school, Ian established a reputation for being something of a problem. He was frequently in trouble at home, at school, and in society at large. Eventually he reached the crossroads of deciding between continuing in this anti-social behaviour or learning how to channel his strength and developing self-control. He joined the US Marine Corps and, through the discipline and encouragement he received there, started on the path which has led to today's success. He served as a demolitions sergeant in Vietnam and eventually received a medical discharge following injuries received while on active service. He then returned to his home town in one of the eastern states of the USA and joined the local operations of a multinational soft drink organisation as a truck jockey. From here he progressed to be a truck driver and, recognising that there was no future without education, went to a community college where he received his associate degree. This led him to a university where he completed his MBA. At the same time his professional career was progressing along with his academic studies and eventually he was appointed Vice President Human Resources for the company. In this role he is active in encouraging others to develop themselves so as to reach their potential.

Ian is one of the most highly motivated people that it has been my pleasure to know. He, his wife, and his sons, practise what is preached relating to personal goal setting and achievement motivation. They tend to be an inspiration to all who know them and, even when the going gets rough, seek to approach issues as problems requiring solution rather than as causes for despondency and despair. Ian's constant thrust is to learn more so that he can become increasingly effective as a husband and father, as a businessman, and as a person who remembers his early beginnings and who seeks to help those in a similar situation to that which he experienced as a teenager.

Motivation from within

There are many myths and legends relating to motivation. In part

management educators have been responsible for this in their propaga-
tion of the functions of managers as being creating, planning, organising, motivating, communicating, and controlling. Such emphasis
has led to a school of thought which argues that motivation can be
externally provided and to the rise of the phenomenon of 'motivational
expert' whose role is to imbue people with drive and enthusiasm so that
their organisations achieve results. All too often the proponents of this
approach create a situation that is analogous to drug addiction. They
encourage their adherents to attend more and more 'motivational'
seminars or workshops with increasing frequency so as to obtain the
desired level of enthusiasm and commitment.

I have no doubt that there is a place for 'motivational' seminars and
workshops but, far too frequently, these are conducted by persons with
questionable qualifications and experience who have discovered that
people are prepared to pay large sums of money to hear an entertaining
and enthusiastic speaker in the hope that it will provide them with
sufficient stimulus to goad them into further achievements.

When one studies the classic writers on motivation, whether they
approach the subject indirectly (eg Freud, Jung, Adler) or directly
(eg Maslow, McGregor, Hertzberg, Atkinson, Aldefer, McClelland
etc) it becomes quite clear that a consistent theme throughout is that
motivation comes from within a person. It is not something that can be
provided by external stimulus. Further, it becomes apparent that there
is no such thing as an unmotivated person. Everybody is motivated.
The question really relates to the end to which such motivation is
channelled. A person may be motivated to work with others or against
them. A person may be motivated to learn in some formal fashion or
not to. A person may be motivated to achieve an organisation's goals
or to thwart that organisation's goals.

I am not simply hair-splitting in this issue. I believe that one of
the tragedies relating to our modern educational process concerns
the issue of motivation. If we approach students from the viewpoint
of them being motivated or not motivated then we will channel our
energies towards 'motivating' these people to learn. This means that
we will look towards such solutions as rewards and punishments – ie
a traditional behaviouristic approach. When this does not work we
will tend to blame the learners rather than query the methodology.
If, however, we approach the issue from the perspective of saying
'these learners/students are motivated but not motivated to learn
under existing circumstances' then we will re-examine the overall
environment in which learning takes place and this will include such
matters as the teaching methodology and philosophy as well as the
issue of rewards and punishments. When this is done we may come to

a significantly different solution than that which is normally reached. It may even be, when we re-phrase the question, that our emphasis may change from promoting education to that of promoting learning!

The principles of learner managed learning are consistent with the philosophy that motivation is an inner drive and that there is no such thing as an unmotivated person. What the education process ought to be about is creating an environment in which people channel their motivational drives towards the goal of learning. This is consistent with Knowles' affirmation that 'the point at which a person takes responsibility for their own growth and development is the point at which they become psychologically an adult.' It is consistent also with the emphasis that Maslow makes that the healthy person is motivated by growth motivation towards self-actualisation rather than by deficiency motivation such as is dealt with by appealing to the safety/security needs of rewards and punishment.

I have referred already to the report to the Club of Rome. In this Botkin, Elamadjara and Malitza (1979:25) refer to the concept of 'anticipatory learning' which they define as '. . . the capacity to face new, possibly unprecedented, situations.' They speak of this as being 'the acid test' for innovative learning processes. It is the ability to deal with the future; to foresee coming events as well as to evaluate the medium-term and long-range consequences of current decisions and actions. They see anticipatory learning as being the inventing or creating of new alternatives where none existed before with the result that rather than reacting and searching for answers when it might be too late to implement solutions we are exhibiting degrees of control over the future by preparing for as many as possible contingencies. This sort of learning is possible only when an individual accepts the locus of control as being within themselves. Such an approach is consistent with the concept of motivation that I am propounding.

Maier (1973:329) looks at the factors which impact on the attaining of high performance or merit and sees these being as shown at Figure 3.

He defines aptitude as being 'natural ability'. Key to the whole issue of training is the premise that behaviour or performance is directly related to the ability and motivation of an individual. Unfortunately, in the real world of education, industry, commerce etc, there seems to be an assumption that people can develop ability regardless of aptitude providing their motivation is high enough. When performance is not obtained, then the appeal is made for these people to be 'motivated'. It is this sort of inadequate thinking that is encouraged by many of the purveyors of 'motivational' seminars and aids.

If we return to Maier's approach then the starting place for considering motivation lies in ascertaining the aptitude a person has

Figure 3 *Relationship between factors influencing an employee's merit.*

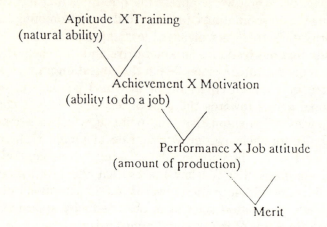

Source: Adapted from Norman R.F. Maier, *Psychology in Industrial Organizations*, Fourth Edition, 1973, Houghton Mifflin Company, p.329. Used with permission.

to perform a particular task or undergo a particular course of study. We do this automatically in some instances. For example there are very few educators or business people who would ask a person with an obvious physical disability to undergo an educational experience or training programme for which their disability showed them to have no aptitude. Yet, when it comes to less obvious disabilities than, say, loss of an arm or leg, we are often guilty of failing to assess aptitude prior to providing training. When this happens we tend to blame the learner rather than ourselves. Classic examples of this relate to dealing with dyslexics, colour-blindness, and similar optical problems.

As a very simple example of how easy it is to be caught in this trap consider the following. At the Centre for Leadership Studies we have interactive video instruction equipment which is operated by the learner touching the screen to progress through the programme. During 1989 we had the managing director of a large public department undergoing training on this equipment. One of the first instructions provided is for the learner to touch a red, green, blue, or yellow box to validate that the right video disk is in the machine. This executive – undoubtedly very intelligent and accomplished – experienced considerable difficulty in proceeding with the programme because he could neither read which box to touch nor determine which was the appropriate box because he suffered from colour-blindness. I put him in a very difficult situation in which to perform simply because I failed to check first that he had the aptitude to distinguish between certain colours. For me to have complained that this man lacked motivation would have been patently absurd. For me to have sought to provide some external motivational stimuli in order to get him to perform would have been even more absurd. The issue of performance had nothing to do with either his motivation or his overall ability. The issue related purely and simply to his basic aptitude for distinguishing between certain colours projected on a screen.

If we are to encourage self-direction in learning then we need to create an environment in which the learner can channel their drives towards the attaining of learning rather than obstructing the learning process. For this to happen then, as with many other issues relating to learner managed learning, we must change the paradigm to one in which we consider creating an environment in which people can apply their motivation rather than one in which we motivate people. Studies which illustrate the impact of creating such an environment date back many years (eg Likert (1961) and Livingstone (1969)). In a more recent study two colleagues of mine, Ian and Cathy Reid, provided a longitudinal study relating to the performance of a football team.

While living in Hobart, Tasmania, they observed the actions of football coaches with both winning and losing teams. They noted that there was a tendency for a team that was not winning to receive a tirade from the coach during half-and quarter-time breaks. This outpouring gave even more instructions as to what they should be doing to win the game. It was the Reids' observation that such tirades tended to have no significant positive impact on the game's result in instances where the team was already exerting its utmost ability to win. In fact, in such instances, the effect of providing such instructions seemed to result in the team making more errors following the intervention than was the case prior to the intervention. They then experimented with one team over a two year period. They introduced what they called 'situational football' which used the principles of situational leadership[1] in terms of assessing the readiness (ie the combination of ability and motivation) of the team and matching the coaching style (ie combination of task and relationship behaviour) to that of the readiness level the team was exhibiting. The results achieved demonstrated quite clearly that where the coach and the team had a high expectation of winning and where the coach deliberately sought to create an environment in which the motivational drive of each player was totally oriented towards winning there was a significantly greater probability that the team would win and the incidence of errors dropped significantly.

Goal setting

One of the aids to a person channelling their motivation is that of goal setting. Maslow's concept of growth motivation (Maslow 1968) requires that a person has some concept of what they can become or achieve and then work towards this. Goal setting is a means of formalising this growth process. In every instance where I have observed learner managed learning being instrumental in obtaining formal qualifications I have noted that the ability to set high but achievable goals has been an essential ingredient for success. But goal setting on its own is not enough. Coupled with the goal setting must be a mechanism for obtaining feedback on those goals. This is the positive contribution of people such as Skinner (1938, 1971, 1974) and the operant conditioning school of behaviourism. Clavell (1963) illustrates this extremely well in the epilogue of his book *The Children's Story*.

That fall she was almost six and she came home from first school – almost first day – and said in a proud rush: 'Daddy, Daddy, listen: I plege illegence to the flag . . .' Her tiny hand was over her heart and when she had finished the blur of words she peered up at me. 'There,' she said breathlessly and held out her hand.
'There what, my darling?'
'You owe me a dime!'
'Oh? What for?'
'The plege illegence. Didn't I say it right? Oh, I'm sure I did. Didn't I?'
'Oh yes, yes, I think you did.' At that time I was not a citizen. 'But why a dime?'
'The teacher said everyone has to learn it and say it and then your dad or mum gives you a dime. That's what the teacher said.'
I paid her.
'Thank you,' she said, very satisfied. 'How about another dime if I say it again?'
'One dime at a time. By the way, what's pledge mean?'
'Huh?'
'Pledge? Allegiance?'
She was perplexed. 'Plege illegence is plege illegence.'
'Didn't your teacher explain what you were learning? Any of those long words?'
Her frown deepened. 'We've to learn it and say it and then we get a dime. That's what our teacher said.' Then she added happily, 'I know I said it right. I was better than Johnny . . .'
During that day I asked all kinds of people of every age, 'You know the I pledge allegiance . . .' but before I could finish, at once they would all parrot it, the words almost always equally blurred. In every case I discovered that no one teacher, ever – or anyone – had ever explained the words to any one of them. Everyone just had to learn to say it.
The Children's Story came into being that day. It was then that I realised how completely vulnerable my child's mind was – any mind for that matter – under controlled circumstances . . .
It pleases me greatly because it keeps asking me questions . . .
Questions like what's the use of 'I pledge allegiance' without understanding? Like

why is it so easy to divest thoughts and implant others? Like what is freedom and why is it so hard to explain?
The Children's Story keeps asking me all sorts of questions I cannot answer.
Perhaps you can – then your child will . . .

I suggest that, among all the other questions that this powerful little story raises, is that of motivation for learning. Clavell's daughter was quite clear. She was learning the Pledge of Allegiance because her teacher had instructed her to and she was told that, should she learn it, she would receive positive reinforcement in terms of a dime from her father. It seems to me that, in a great many instances our motivation for learning is not dissimilar from that of Clavell's daughter. People attend classes to obtain sufficient knowledge to pass examinations. They are there because, in Skinner's terms, there is positive reinforcement available because of a piece of paper or a job. In many instances the knowledge that they have of the subject is marginal to say the least.

This can be illustrated from my own experiences. In November 1967 I was sitting the final examinations for my Diploma in Divinity and, by dint of the examination schedule, I happened to have one three-hour examination on the Friday afternoon and the final examination on Saturday morning. Both subjects interested me and there were several days' gap between these two examinations and the one preceding them. However, as is not uncommon, I was more proficient in one subject than the other. It happened that the subject in which I had less competency was the one on Friday afternoon. I decided to spend the days prior to that examination concentrating on revision of that subject and to trust on last-minute cramming to revise for the final subject. I finished the Friday examination at 5.30 pm and returned to my study. I worked all night at revising my material and, after only a very short amount of sleep, I went into the examination at 9.30 on Saturday morning. I passed both examinations and completed my diploma but, to this day, I cannot be sure as to what the two subjects were, nor have I any recollection of the subject matter examined. My motivation for learning was purely and simply to pass that examination and so complete the diploma. I was not seriously interested in what the Club of Rome Report would call the 'anticipatory learning' aspect of those subjects.

In the period since 1967 I have taught in many universities and colleges of advanced education in Australia, New Zealand, and the United States. Without exception I have found the main thrust of the teaching both to assume and encourage a motivation that is geared to the obtaining of, in the Club of Rome's terms, maintenance learning and a piece of paper or other formal recognition. The goal setting and the reinforcement are geared not towards growth motivation but towards deficiency motivation and so become ends in themselves rather than part of the overall process of being.

Jackson and Prosser (1986) suggest that this is one of the key problems experienced by our graduates from high school and university when they enter the work force. During their formal educational period they have learnt that their interests lie in obtaining grades not an education. Consequently, although our students are bright and do much work as defined by the system, little thought is given to the possibility that they might do even better or more useful work and be better prepared for later life. We should be seeking to produce graduates who know how to learn independently and also in co-operation with other people. What this means is that we should be encouraging a paradigm in which learners have a desire to be able to cope with a range of problems and issues and learn within an environment that enables them to assess whether or not they are doing this satisfactorily. Jackson and Prosser are not alone in this. Bock (1986) argues that the same is true in the United States. The argument made by these writers is that educational goals should be expressed as competencies rather than as obtaining grades *per se*. By so doing it will help people to develop effective communication skills; to develop the ability to make judgement values; to develop awareness and understanding of the contemporary world; and to develop an understanding of and sensitivity towards the arts and a knowledge of the humanities; as well as improving analytical abilities, strengthening problem-solving capacities, and achieving understanding of the relationship between the individual and the environment.

Sullivan (1986:534) looks at the differing theories of human nature and the way in which these affect organisations. He draws a distinction between democratic man (in which human nature is viewed as compelling humans to seek to perfect themselves by freely pursuing their individual self-interests), modern man (in which humans are compelled by physical, chemical, psychological, and social 'laws' to be influenced in any number of complex ways), totalitarian man (which is based on the assumption that there is no independent force of law or will or reason inside most humans which is powerful enough to control transient feelings, emotions, and passions of the moment, – it is up to the State, its organisations, and the elites which own the State to control the masses so that anarchic behaviour gives way to ordered existence) and hermeneutic man. The hermeneutic model is a process view of human nature in which a human is a 'becoming' rather than a 'being' and it easily associates itself with the characterising of humans as self-creating, sense-making, active, and interactive. This concept of the nature of man is totally compatible with a learner managed approach to learning and general self-development. In this model the motivation to learn comes from within because the bounds of one's nature are self-imposed rather than imposed by external forces. Sullivan argues (page 542):

> What these concepts mean for a model of human-kind in organisations is that humans are seen as creators of organisational reality and structures rather than as responders to them. Managing becomes interacting to achieve erlebnis (lived experiences) rather than merely endured experiences in the organisation.

That this is a different philosophy of the nature of man and human motivation from that which is espoused by traditional pedagogical approaches is obvious. In the traditional approach we are seeking to bring about change by being an external force which offers the goal of passing an examination, pleasing a teacher, or some other goal whereas in the self-directed approach the learner has taken responsibility for his or her own learning and change process because it is something which comes out of themselves. In this regard the person-centred approach by Rogers in both psychotherapy and education (Rogers 1961, 1970) is in accord with the hermeneutical model.

Throughout Sullivan's argument it is possible to substitute the word 'learners' or 'students' for 'workers' and 'professor' or 'teacher' for 'manager'. When this is done then his argument makes sense for the educational and learning process. Equally it explains many of the motivational problems faced in traditional educational environments as, with the emphasis on maintenance learning, there are many instances when the learning process and subject matter fails to make any sense to the learner and the manipulation of outcomes and conditions have only a low correlation with desired work performance.

Vroom (1964) posited the expectancy theory of motivation which, in brief, says:

1. Behaviour is determined by a combination of forces in the individual and in the environment.
2. Individuals make conscious decisions about their own behaviour.
3. Individuals have different needs, desires, and goals.
4. Individuals decide among alternative behaviours based on their expectation that a given behaviour will lead to a desired outcome.

I believe that this model has much to say in terms of motivation and learner managed learning. In fact I argue elsewhere (Long 1989) that we cannot obtain desired performance whether as individuals or as managers unless we take into account the expectancies that relate to this performance. The difference between the application of the expectancy model in the modernist view and the hermeneutical view lies in the setting of goals and in the drive towards them as well as in the perceived results. In the modernistic approach this is primarily external whereas in the hermeneutical approach it is primarily internal and may have no obvious influence from external sources.

Facilitating achievement motivation

All of this reinforces my argument that we are unable to motivate other people. Our role in all areas of life is to provide an environment in which people can motivate themselves. If we fail to provide this environment then we have the effect of removing motivation from people; of making them reliant on us or other outside sources for goals, direction, and feedback. When such an approach fails to achieve the desired results we are quick to place the blame on the individual rather than ourselves. In the educational arena we appear to have forgotten such writers as McGregor (1960:10) who says:

> Another fallacy is often revealed in managerial attempts to control human behaviour. When we fail to achieve the results we desire, we tend to seek the cause everywhere but where it usually lies; in our choice of inappropriate methods of control. The engineer does not blame water for flowing downhill rather than up, nor gases for expanding rather than contracting when heated. However, when people respond to managerial decisions in undesired ways, the normal response is to blame them. It is their stupidity, or their uncooperativeness, or their laziness which is seized on as the explanation of what happened, not management's failure to select appropriate means for control.

For too long we have placed the blame for low levels of learning, inadequate performance, behavioural problems in the educational environment, and the like on the student rather than on the professor. The time has come when we must look inward to ascertain our value system as to the nature of man and the motivational process. If we believe that our role is to manipulate situations and students so that they obtain maintenance learning then we will continue to use a primarily pedagogical approach. If, however, we subscribe to the hermeneutical view in which we are seeking to develop self-reliance and self-ownership for the learning and growth process then we we will move towards andragogy and learner managed learning. In this approach we will endeavour to assist our learners to experience education as a lived experience. That this places considerably more strain on a professor and requires significantly more work than a straight lecturing approach is not disputed. The result, however, will be highly motivated learners who take responsibility for their own learning process and individual growth. The motivation within them for reaching their potential will be encouraged rather than stifled and learning will become an exciting experience rather than a drudgery to be avoided as soon as one can get out of the educational system. When this occurs we will have moved a long way towards assisting the development of Maslow's growth motivation.

It is this sort of emphasis that is made by McClelland (1966) in which he examines the phenomena of some people being 'challenged by opportunity and willing to work hard to achieve'. It is this concept of 'achievement motivation' (which McClelland contrasts with power motivation and affiliation motivation) which comes closest to Maslow's viewpoint of growth motivation as being appropriate for healthy people. Central to lifelong learning and development is the obtaining of a sense of achievement coupled with a desire for further growth and achievement. This can only come from inside a person and cannot be induced by external stimuli. The best that external forces can do is to create an environment in which achievement motivation can operate.

This is what made the difference to Ian. While at school the total emphasis was on rewards and punishment. He experienced all the traditional approaches taken by the behavioural school in that he received positive and negative reinforcement for acts of omission and commission. Rather than modifying his behaviour Ian learnt to avoid punishment and to devise mechanisms by which he would not be caught. It was not until he encountered an environment which stressed the ability to achieve and in which it was made possible for him to achieve that a change occured in his behaviour. Now for over twenty years Ian has experienced growth. He sees himself constantly as becoming rather than being and he creates an environment in which his family, those people with whom he works, and members of society can also obtain this sense of achievement and experience the positive impact of growth motivation in their quest for lifelong learning and development.

Note:

1. 'Situational Leadership' is a registered trade mark of the Centre for Leadership Studies and Leadership Studies International.

8 A Learner Managed Learning Model

Case study: *What and how?*

Helen is in her mid-30s. Her educational and work background has been varied. She left school at age 15 and was involved in clerical work for many years. Although a good worker she found it difficult to remain with any employer for protracted periods and, in her first fifteen years of working, she had worked for seventeen different employers. At around age 30 Helen's current employer suggested that, rather than leave, she should seek job satisfaction in another area of the company. The result was that Helen moved into sales and here she found her niche. Currently she is sales manager in a company selling intangibles.

In 1986 Helen came to me to discuss her future career prospects. She was concerned about her future and she wanted to undertake a series of learning experiences that would better equip her for career development. It was her hope that, ultimately, she would be able to complete a degree and move into an area providing counselling services to disadvantaged people.

Helen had reached the point of recognising she must take responsibility for her own growth and development. She could see the problem and knew where the answer lay. However, she was scared that her past bad experiences in education would be repeated and she sought to discover how she could become involved in a learning process that was different from the ones she knew.

Self-management

My argument to date has been that we need to change our paradigm away from learning being a passive experience through to the situation where people take responsibility for their own growth and development. I have quoted Knowles who defines learner managed learning as:

That process in which individuals take the initiative, with or without the help of others, in diagnosing their learning needs, formulating learning goals, identifying human and material resources for learning, choosing and implementing learning strategies, and evaluating learning outcomes.

Further I have referred to Knowles' statement that the point at which an individual takes responsibility for their own growth and development is the point at which they become essentially adult. In building up my argument I have sought to provide an overview of learning theory and to contrast recurrent education with lifelong learning. From here I have moved to consider the environment in which learner managed learning can occur and the difference between the teaching of adults and the teaching of children. I have looked at the dichotomies that tend to occur between behavioural approaches to teaching and cognitive approaches and, in addition, I have discussed the issues of power and motivation as they relate to the learning process. My intention throughout has been to lay a base onto which can be built the learner managed learning model so that, from this model, we can then consider the applications of the model in both the corporate context and the general educational sphere.

As we develop the learner managed learning model it is important to note first that the control for learning must move from the teacher or facilitator to the learner. Worell and Nelson (1974:33) in discussing the concept of self-management argue that the ultimate goal with children should be to move the locus of control away from adults and onto the child. We know that the development of independent self-management is a complex process. We know also that we have still much to learn about this process. But, no matter how much we must yet learn, we do know that self-regulation develops as a companion process of effective external contingency control.

For a child to develop self-management there are four things required. These are:

1.   Self-observation.
2.   Goal setting.
3.   Self-instruction.
4.   Self-evaluation.

Self-observation

Many people have considerable difficulty in observing behaviour. What happens is that we interpret what we see and extrapolate this so that our observations become confused with our deductions. I see this consistently when I am approached by managers, parents, and educators who tell me that someone they know has 'an attitude problem'. What they are really saying is that they have observed behaviour which they consider to be unacceptable. Because this behaviour is unacceptable they are assuming that the person involved does not want to behave in an acceptable manner. They are observing behaviour but, rather than commenting on the behaviour, they are extrapolating from that to draw conclusions about a person's frame of mind. In a totally different sphere, police friends of mine have, for a long time, used the phrase 'lying like an eye-witness'. What they mean by this is not that witnesses deliberately lie. In fact they believe that witnesses very seldom deliberately lie. What happens however is that they see, for example, the actual accident and then extrapolate from that how the accident must have occurred. Accordingly, for some witnesses to have actually seen what they believed they saw, they would have needed two heads, both facing different ways, and four eyes.

It is this sort of problem that prompts Merrill and Reid (1981:33) to call for us to remove the subjectiveness out of our observations. By this they mean that, if we are going to learn to observe effectively we will need to rid ourselves of words and phrases that describe the inadequacies of a person or which describe our own reactions, feelings, and judgements about a person. They go on (p34) to provide the chart shown at Table 1 as an example of objective observation *vis-a-vis* value judgements and personal traits.

If people are going to get involved in learner managed learning they will need to learn to observe and discriminate their own behaviour. They will need to learn to be objective in this and to focus on the behaviour itself in very specific terms. We must learn to look at actual behaviour rather than generalising about what we think may or may not have occurred.

Goal setting

While it is true that many people do set goals for themselves, I suggest that the vast majority of people allow life to drift along with them remaining reactive to situations rather than seeking to take control. Goal setting requires that a person seeks to make things happen. The poet Longfellow once said 'In this world a man is either a hammer or an anvil'. Goal setting is all about being a hammer. It means that we are taking responsibility for shaping those things that happen to us rather than being the anvil around which things are shaped. We must teach learners to set reasonable goals. When a person learns that small goals with frequent rewards for successful accomplishment can provide a step-by-step progress towards result achievement, there tends to be a movement towards goal setting in most areas of life. An important issue relating to this is that, as an individual becomes more accustomed to goal setting and achieving results, there needs to be a transition away

Table 1 *Common ways of describing people.* (Limit descriptions to type of words in column two to describe behaviour objectively.)

ONE Inner Qualities, Traits, or Characteristics	TWO Interpersonal Situations	THREE Reactions, Feelings, and Judgments
Honest	Loud • Quiet	I like him
Intelligent	Fast-paced • Slow-paced	She bugs me
Ambitious	Facially • Facially animated controlled	She interests me
Motivated	Inflected • Monotone speech speech	He seems nice
Interested	Rigid posture • Casual posture	He's strange
Sincere	Direct • Indirect eye contact eye contact	I hate him
Hypocritical	Dramatic speech • Factual speech	I trust her
	▲ These descriptions identify (1) an interpersonal situation in which two or more people interact; and (2) observable behavior which can be described by an observer and verified by observations made by others.	

Source: From David W. Merrill, Roger H. Reid *Personal Styles and Effective Performance*, 1981, Chilton Book Company, Radnor, Pennsylvania, Page 34. Used with permission.

from external rewards and reinforcement to internal self-rewards and reinforcement for achievement. In other words, in terms of Maslow's growth motivation, there needs to be a move away from deficiency need satisfaction to growth need satisfaction or towards the process of self-actualisation.

Blanchard and Lorber (1984) talk about the need for goal setting to be done properly. They see this as happening when the desired performance is stated in behavioural terms – that is, it can be seen (observed) and counted (measured).

Locke (1968) looked at the role intention plays in human behaviour and argues that many motivational theories ignored goal setting and, in later works (Locke 1975, 1977) he speaks of these as nothing more than 'cognitive hedonism'. Locke feels that people strive to attain goals in order to satisfy their emotions and desires. To him goals provide a directional nature to people's behaviour and guide their thoughts and actions to one outcome rather than another. When we set goals then we respond and perform according to these intentions or goals even if the goal itself is not attained.

Many people have trouble with goal setting because they seek to achieve too much at one time. Kouzes and Posner (1987) tell the story of Donald Bennett who, on July 15, 1982, realised one of his lifelong dreams of standing on the summit of Mount Rainier. Bennett became the first amputee to scale that 14,410 foot mountain and, when asked how he did it, explained 'one hop at a time. I imagined myself on top of that mountain one thousand times a day in my mind. But when I started to climb it, I just said to myself, "anyone can hop from here to there." And I would. And when the going got roughest, and I was really exhausted, that's when I would look down at the path ahead and say to myself, "You just have to take one more step, and anybody can do that." And I would.'

This is the core of goal setting. It is the action of breaking down our visions and desires into step-by-step pieces that we know can be achieved. When we do this properly then one step leads logically to the next step and so we continue to climb the mountain and work towards our vision or dream with the knowledge that, even if it is not ultimately attained, we have at least been involved in the process of making something happen – ie the process of becoming – and this is the growth motivation or self-actualisation process of which Maslow spoke.

Self-instruction

This is very closely allied with the goal setting aspect. In this area an individual needs to develop the skills which will enable them to determine the instructional techniques that they will find most appropriate.

In Chapter 5 I reproduced the diagram provided by Wolfe and Kolb in their graphic illustration of the experiential model for growth and development. Kolb, Rubin and McIntyre (1984) argue that effective learners rely on four different learning modes. These are concrete experience (CE), reflective observation (RO), abstract conceptualisation (AC), and active experimentation (AE). By this they mean that effective learners must be able to involve themselves fully, openly, and without bias in new experiences (CE); they must be able to reflect on and observe these experiences from many perspectives (RO); they must be able to create concepts that integrate their observations into logically sound theories (AC); and they must be able to use these theories to make decisions and solve problems (AE).

In this model they do not see people as necessarily being equally comfortable or capable with each of these different steps. They argue that each of us has weaknesses and strengths in various of these areas but that we will have a bias towards the one with which we feel most comfortable. Accordingly a learning style inventory has been developed by David Kolb to enable us to understand our key orientations. (Kolb, Rubin and McIntyre (1984)).

Wolfe and Kolb (1984:130) argue that as a result of heredity, life-experience, and demands of our present society most people develop learning styles that emphasise some learning abilities over others. As a result of these we come to an individual balance between active and reflective learning, and between immediate and analytical processing of learning. This leads them to suggest that a person will tend towards one of the following learning styles:

- The converger whose dominant learning abilities are abstract conceptualisation and active experimentation. This person's greatest strength lies in the practical application of ideas.
- The diverger whose dominant learning abilities are concrete experience and reflective observation. The greatest strength of this person lies in their imaginative ability and they excel in the ability to view concrete situations from many perspectives and, for this reason, to perform well in situations that call for generation of ideas.
- The assimilator whose dominant learning abilities are abstract conceptualisation and reflective observation. This person's greatest strength lies in their ability to create theoretical models and they excel in inductive reasoning and in assimilating disparate observations into an integrated explanation.

- The accommodator whose dominant learning abilities are concrete experience and active experimentation. The greatest strength for this person lies in doing things and carrying out plans and experiments that involve them in new experiences. This person tends to be more of a risk taker than the other three styles.

Part of our role as facilitators should be to assist people to understand the way in which they best learn and to assist them in obtaining learning experiences that are compatible with this learning style. When this is done it is far more likely that a person will be able to make the move to self-instruction rather than relying primarily on instruction from other people.

Self-evaluation

For learner managed learning to work, an individual needs to take responsibility for evaluating their progress towards various goals. In many ways this summarises the previous three points. Self-evaluation requires that people can honestly observe their own behaviour and, without rationalising or indulging in wishful thinking, be totally honest as to whether or not their behaviour is appropriate to achieve the goals that have been set. They need to learn to pace themselves and to keep designated records to ensure that goals will be met within the appropriate time frame. Obviously coupled with this is the need for them to determine their own system of positive reinforcement so as to facilitate the growth that they are seeking.

To fulfil this aspect requires significant maturity on behalf of the learner. This is consistent with Knowles' comment that the point at which a person takes responsibility for their own growth and development is the point at which they become essentially adult. Appropriate self-evaluation requires a willingness and an ability to accept responsibility for one's own actions and to be pro-active in terms of one's development. This is central to learner managed learning.

Zemke (1981) suggests that learning and teaching theories 'function better as a resource than as a Rosetta Stone.' They see the humanistic, behavioural, cognitive, and developmental approaches as all being of valuable guidance when matched with an appropriate learning task and go on to argue that the trainer of adults needs to take an eclectic approach rather than a single theory-based approach to developing strategies and procedures. As we move on to develop the learner managed learning model it will become clear that an eclectic approach is essential for learner managed learning to be effective but that the emphasis at any stage should be determined by the learner rather than by the facilitator. In learner managed learning the learner must be free to choose whatever approach is most suitable in terms of the requirements of the actual learning experience.

The four parts of learner managed learning

To my mind any model for learner managed learning must include four distinct segments.

1. Self-assessment
2. Goal setting
3. Action plans
4. Assessment of progress

Self-assessment

It is my observation that most people encounter various stages at which they are faced with their present situation and encounter questions as to how they got to that point and where the future is leading. Unfortunately, again from observation, it appears as though this period of introspection becomes a factor leading to depression rather than a stimulus to growth.

Kolb and Boyatzis (1984:108) argue that successful change is a function of one's ability to maintain awareness of the dissidence between one's ideal self and one's current self. For many people this is the hardest part of the entire learner managed learning process. It is not that they are unwilling to do self-assessment but, in the majority of instances, they have never before been involved in assessment that is designed to facilitate growth.

There are a variety of tools available to facilitate this process and publications such as those produced by University Associates[1] include a wide selection of these. In my own work with people who are interested in learner managed learning I have found the following approach to be effective:

> Spend some time thinking about your life. Now write a brief biography (up to three or four pages) that talks about your family, your education, your experiences to date, and where you see yourself as being today. When you have completed this, write a second biography in which you idealise what may have happened and, sometimes probably wish had happened, had you taken advantage of every opportunity that had been presented to you. When you have completed this, consider the factors that were involved in influencing you not to take advantage of every available opportunity you had. Over which of these factors did you have some control but, for a variety of reasons, either chose not to use that control or failed to see that you had control at that time?

The final stage of this assessment is to assess where you are now (the actual not the idealised) and where you would like to be in the next five years. Consider the opportunities currently available to you and consider the factors which are impacting upon those opportunities. Over which of these could you exert some control? What alternatives do you have in regard to exerting influence on any of these factors?

When this exercise is completed I spend time with the learner discussing what they have written. We examine the extent to which behaviour is being observed or inferences are being drawn from behaviour. My experience has been that the people who are most prepared to be honest during this phase are those who have the greatest probability of success on a learner managed learning programme. Very often I find that the learner needs some assistance in this exercise and, as appropriate, I have suggested that we complete the exercise by means of discussion with them tape recording the entire process. What I am endeavouring to do is to increase self-awareness and to start the process of learning how to observe behaviour. Obviously, too, by such self-evaluation, there is a base laid for future self-assessment of progress.

Goal setting

Central to goal setting is the need to create an environment for success. Many of the people with whom I work have experienced questionable levels of success, if not downright failure, in their previous educational and learning processes. Consequently they have a fear of failure in this venture. In such an instance I find it important to explore previous successes experienced by the prospective learner and to discuss how these came about and whether or not there is a common thread between them. Invariably, once a person starts to accept that they have had successes and they have influenced those successes it becomes possible to facilitate in a goal-setting process that is designed for success experiences. A key factor in this requires that the starting point is within the learner's boundaries of psychological safety with any movement outside these bounds being gradual and low-risk. Invariably, the greater the perception of risk which the learner has of the learning process the less likely they are to embark upon learner managed learning.

A number of key issues generally become apparent during this goal setting phase. Almost always there arises an early awareness of the need to select between competing goals. The choice is not necessarily between a positive goal and a negative goal but, more often, is between two positive goals – both of which are achievable but which are mutually exclusive. In the early stages a learner may be unprepared to give up an alternative goal and, in such instances,

I suggest that action paths leading to both goals be prepared and explored with the intention that, at a later stage, we return to the start of divergence between the goals and make a decision as to which is the more appropriate one to pursue. Sometimes this requires a prioritising as to the desirability of each anticipated goal but, almost always, this is not possible at the early stages.

In Chapter 3 I explored the environment for learner managed learning. At this goal setting phase it is very important to examine the environment in which the learner managed learning process will occur. There are significant differences between a learner managed learning programme that will take place primarily in a corporate context as opposed to one that will take place primarily in a traditional educational context. At this stage it will become necessary to consider the parameters within which learner managed learning may or may not be possible as well as the general resources available for the learning process.

A key component at this stage is to develop an expectation of success in the mind of the learner and to work on building up their confidence. They need to remain fully cognisant that learner managed learning is an ongoing process rather than a particular content – it is 'becoming' not 'being' – and, accordingly, there are no right or wrong answers. Because they are setting their own goals the criteria for rightness or wrongness are simply those criteria which they themselves choose to apply in their own self-development. This can be a very scary concept for people who are used to relying on external loci of control.

Action plans

It is at this point that the work previously completed is put into a structured form. Now is the time for checking that no step is so big that there is a greater likelihood of failure than there is of success and for a careful appraisal of the goal sequence. At this stage, also, the learning strategies are set out in detail together with listing bibliographies and reading lists, sources of learning experiences, general resources, and the like.

I encourage learners to structure this section in such a way as to ensure clear cut-off points between goals and to approach each goal in the overall hierarchy as an individual phase even though it is interrelated with all other phases.

The action plan stage is extremely important. By determining a hierarchy of goals and mapping out the way by which these goals are to be attained the learner is heightening the probability of success. Done properly it ensures that it shows both the preferred set of actions for attaining any particular goal but includes a fall-back position (or series of fall-back positions) if the preferred action plan is not possible. The key throughout is that every goal should be perceived by the learner as being realistic, achievable, and measurable.

Assessment of progress

I believe it is essential in the learner managed learning process that the learner sets up a series of formal and informal progress checks. Learner managed learning requires a very high level of self-discipline. It is questionable as to whether the most difficult aspect is the phase of starting on the process or continuing on the process. In the period to 1990 I have had involvement with some 200 people who were either interested in a learner managed learning programme or had decided to embark upon a learner managed learning programme. Of this group 146 have sought an undergraduate or graduate degree through learner managed learning processes. As at the time of writing (January 1990) 37 have completed their degrees, a further 60 are still working on their degrees, and the balance have either opted out of a degree programme or have reverted to a traditional university programme because they were unable to cope with the exigencies of learner managed learning.

A common thread throughout all of these is that of self-discipline and self-assessment. In every instance where the degree has been completed the learner has set up an effective process for self-assessment and has been rigid in applying self-discipline procedures to ensure that goals are met. Without exception the extent to which these procedures were followed determined the facility with which the goals were reached. Also, so far as I can ascertain, without exception those who have opted out of the learner managed learning process have found themselves unable to apply the degree of self-discipline required and to follow the assessment procedures set out in their action plan.

Unless specific check points are incorporated in a learner managed learning programme it is possible for the programme to drift without results being attained and, ultimately, for the programme to be a failure. Without check points, by the time slippage is discovered, so much time may have elapsed that effective remedial action is not possible. These assessment points must come in at any point where a detour is possible and, in addition, they must be clearly delineated at every point where it is anticipated a goal will have been reached.

Learner managed learning is results oriented. It is a process in which the learner is determining a set of performance goals and then mapping out a means by which those performance goals can be met. If one waits until after those goals should have been met and then endeavours to ascertain why failure occurred then the learner managed learning process is doomed to failure as one becomes involves in rationalising the reasons for failure and justifying ones actions in the light of failure. A proper means of ongoing assessment built into the learner managed learning programme makes it possible constantly to monitor the inputs available to the learner and the process through which the learner is passing so that these can be modified as required in order to ensure the performance goals are met.

Responsibility

There is one other aspect to the learner managed learning model. This has been referred to in many places throughout the preceding chapters and even within this chapter. It is to stress that, in learner managed learning, the learner is taking responsibility for the learning process. The locus of control must be within the learner and, no matter what assistance they may seek in order to facilitate the self-assessment, the setting of goals, the developing of actions plans, and the institution of assessment, the initiative for all of this must ultimately come from the learner. They must take the leading role in determining what is to be learned, how it is to be learned, and all other variables impacting on the learning process. They may choose to attend lectures, to be involved in such processes as computer-based learning, attendance at seminars or workshops, or any other mechanism with which they feel comfortable and which suits their dominant learning style. The key thing is that, throughout, they are central to controlling this process rather than relying on some external agency of teacher, professor, facilitator, trainer, or whoever to direct them as to what is to be done and how it is to be done.

If we consider a model of learning as requiring a combination of input or didactic behaviour and reinforcement or supportive behaviour then, using a simple standard model in which didactic behaviour and supportive behaviour are seen as independent but interrelated variables it becomes possible to describe teaching strategies in terms that show the interaction of these variables. This is shown diagrammatically at Figure 4.

As can be seen from Figure 4 we can describe teaching strategies in terms of large amounts of didactic behaviour and small amounts of supporting behaviour, large amounts of both didactic behaviour and supportive behaviour, low amounts of didactic behaviour and large amounts of supportive behaviour, and low amounts of both supportive

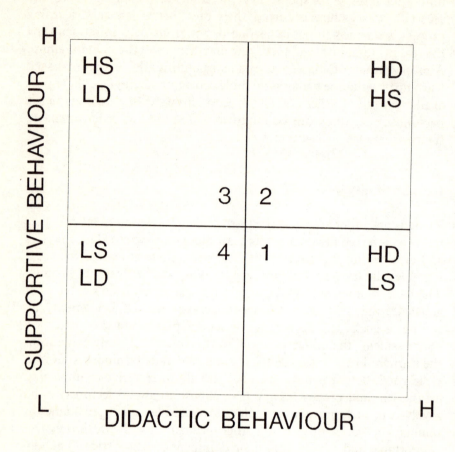

Figure 4 *Relationship between didactic behaviour and supportive behaviour in teaching strategies*

behaviour and didactive behaviour. Keynote words which can be used to describe each of these four quadrants are:

- High didactic behaviour and low supportive behaviour: instructing
- High didactic behaviour and high supportive behaviour: explaining
- Low didactic behaviour and high supportive behaviour: facilitating
- Low didactic behaviour and low supportive behaviour: responding

It is clear also from this sort of approach that a transition arises from a behavioural approach through to a cognitive approach as one moves through the four quadrants.

The question arises as to when it is appropriate to use each of these behaviours. In considering this I am indebted to the work of Hersey and

Blanchard (1988) and their work on situational leadership. No matter what criticisms may be levied against situational leadership theory it is true as Yukl (1989:108) says: 'Hersey and Blanchard reminded us that it is essential to treat different subordinates differently and to treat the same subordinate differently as the situation changes. Moreover, they advanced the important proposition that leaders should be aware of opportunities to build the skill and confidence of subordinates and not just assume that a particular subordinate with deficiencies and skills or motivation must forever remain a "problem employee".'

In considering this approach to learner managed learning we can consider the readiness of the learner as the key determinant of the appropriate style to use in teaching strategy. If we describe learner readiness as four ranges – R1 through R4 – we can see those ranges moving from the point where a student is uninformed and insecure through to the point where they are knowledgeable and confident. Thus the ranges become:

- R1 – uninformed/insecure
- R2 – uninformed/confident
- R3 – knowledgeable/insecure
- R4 – knowledgeable/confident

Following through from this then it again becomes clear that when a person is at an R1 or R2 level of readiness the strategy should be primarily teacher-centred but as a person moves through an R3 or R4 level of readiness the teaching strategy should move towards a learner-centred approach.

When we put the teacher strategy and the readiness of learner together then we obtain a model as shown at Figure 5.

Considering this in terms of learner managed learning it becomes apparent that the emphasis of teaching strategy should be aimed at moving a person or encouraging the movement of a person from an R1 through to an R4 level of readiness in any particular subject or topic. Accordingly the curve which moves from quadrant 1 through to quadrant 4 is one which simply shows a movement of strategy and shift of emphasis from a teacher-centred approach through to a learner-centred approach over an agreed time-frame. This is only possible if the matters referred to earlier in this chapter receive appropriate attention. Early in the learning process we should be encouraging learners to take responsibility for self-assessment, goal setting, action-plans, and assessment of progress so that, even from very earliest days, we are implementing some aspect of andragogy – a concept that is totally in accord with that advocated by Knowles (1984:54) to which reference is made in Chapter 4.

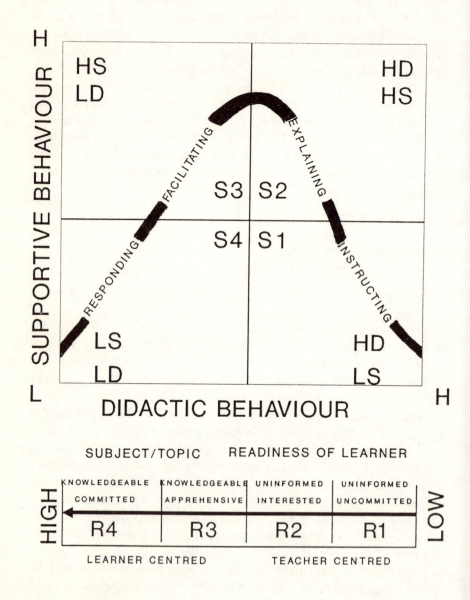

TEACHING STRATEGIES

Figure 5 *The Combination of teaching strategies and learner readiness*

Helen went through this process. When first she came to me for assistance she had expected I would provide her with a clear action plan and take the initiative in showing her what to do and how to do it. Certainly we spent a lot of time discussing what learner managed learning was all about, but, finally, she came to the realisation that if she was to embark upon such a process she had to take responsibility for control. This she did and, at the time of writing, she is completing the second year of a PhD programme. The evidence to date is such that she can be expected to graduate with top marks as a result of her learner managed learning programme.

Note:

1   University Associates
     7596 Eades Avenue
     La Jolla
     California 92037

9 Learner Managed Learning in a Corporate Context

Case study: *Is there a difference?*

All through his schooling, Eric knew that he wanted to be a school teacher. On graduating from high school he went to university and completed his Masters Degree in Education. From here he spent several years as a high school teacher prior to joining the Army Education Corps. After five years in the army he joined a university as a senior lecturer in the teacher training faculty. Here he was instrumental in setting up a new diploma course as well as teaching on the Bachelors of Education programme. At age 35 Eric felt that he should make the transition from the educational sphere into training within business and industry. He joined a small training consultancy as a senior consultant with responsibility both to conduct training programmes and generate new business.

Eric commenced his new job with enthusiasm. He was an extremely competent trainer and he enjoyed working with a wider age range and experience range of people than was the case at the university. But within three months Eric had left the consultancy and was selling life insurance. The transition from a university environment to the consultancy was too great for him.

Eventually Eric moved into the training department with a large organisation and became a highly successful commercial trainer. There were times when he didn't think he'd make it.

Introduction

For many years now my work in the field of organisational behaviour has been both within the formal educational system and in the wider world of public and private sector business and industry training. Since 1976 I have been involved primarily with management training outside of the formal educational system, with brief forays as a guest or visiting professor or, at best, part-time teaching within university environments. For that reason many of the examples drawn and emphases made relate to business and industry rather than to pure research or academia.

Learning can and does take place in any environment. The institutional model of learning presumes a shared definition of objectives in the classroom and an imbalance of expertise between facilitator and trainee. There is a temptation for persons to argue that learning must occur in such an environment and, perhaps for this reason, many people equate learning with education. Sometimes there is a failure to realise not only does learning also take place outside the bounds of the traditional classroom but, particularly with adult learners, the classroom situation is becoming increasingly outmoded. This is an issue that will be explored further in Chapter 10 but, even within the corporate context, sometimes it is assumed that the important learning is done within the formal training context rather than seeing such a context as being only part of the overall learning experience. Ideally all learning within a corporate context (ie whether intentional or incidental) will be consistent as regards the philosophy and objectives of that organisation. If this is to occur then the role of training must be taken out of the hands of a few select professional trainers and placed in the hands of every line manager and supervisor. It must become the responsibility of every person in authority to accept responsibility for facilitating the growth of the people answering to him or her. On the other side of the coin it will become necessary to encourage individual responsibility by employees at all levels so that they are pro-active as regards their need for learning experiences.

Within the corporate context any learning programme must take into account three things:

1. The present state or position of the corporation.
2. Corporate goals and strategies.
3. The present level of knowledge and skills of each employee.

The present state or position of the corporation

The day has long since gone when an organisation could consider itself in anything other than an open systems model. Although, at times, it appears as though organisations act as though they are independent from their environment the truth is that the organisation which ignores any aspect of the environment within which it operates is an organisation doomed to failure.

Far too often I encounter the situation where an organisation is training people for the future using technologies of the present but based on requirements of the past. One such technical area is the example of airlines who continued to train people as flight engineers even though the planes on which these people would be flying required a pilot and co-pilot only and the flight engineer's role had become largely superfluous. In Australia at least this has led to industrial disputation where the trade unions still seek to insist on having three persons in the cockpit even though the manufacturers recommendations and designs are for two person cockpits only.

History is essential. In fact it has been said that a person without history has nothing. However, whether or not this is philosophically arguable, there is no doubt that the present state of a person is infinitely more important than the past. People who dwell on past successes or failures tend to be of little or no value in the present-day world. We cannot say that because something has occurred in the past everything in the future must be oriented towards it. This is akin to a parent saying that, because Tommy once had bronchitis as a baby, he is constantly 'delicate' and therefore cannot be involved in strenuous sports or outdoor activities as he grows through puberty into adolescence. Rather than recognising normal growth and development, the parent seeks to act as though the child has remained an invalid. In this regard the parent is basing their present actions on a past situation and, all too often, this does little or nothing to prepare the child for adult life.

The same is true of corporations. Many organisations seem to feel that because they have achieved certain things in the past then the present should be measured in the light of these achievements. While it is true that achievements of the past should not be forgotten and that failures of the past should be seen as warning signals and lessons, it is the present that is of paramount importance. We should be preparing for the future based on what is happening today not on what has happened in the past. Accordingly it is essential for an organisation to have a very clear picture of where it is today if it is to formulate any goals and strategies.

In learner managed learning an organisation, prior to embarking upon training, must undertake some form of survey that shows its present position with respect to all positions and people within the organisation. Too many organisations seem to feel that they should rush into a training programme without definitely ascertaining the present state of the organisation and determining whether or not a training programme is required or instead is a luxury. When training that is not required is provided then participants quickly become disillusioned with the organisation and its human resource development function. When this occurs there is a tendency to equate the training function with all bad experiences from the years of formal education to the end that training becomes written-off as irrelevant or a waste of time.

In order to deal with this issue it is my practice to recommend an organisation conducts an organisational audit or, as the Center for Leadership Studies calls it, an organisational x-ray. The purpose of this is to examine the causal, intervening, and end-variables of an organisation so as to isolate problem areas and ascertain the best possible means of dealing with these. Let me illustrate what I mean by these variables.

Any operation be it government or non-government, for profit or not for profit, business or social, etc has three key components. These components are the inputs to that organisation; the way in which these inputs are processed or handled; and the outputs of that organisation. As a very simple example we can consider the inputs of a family to comprise the parents and children, the processes to be the way in which the parents fulfil their parenting role, and the outputs to be whether or not the children grow to be healthy independent adults. A more complex example could be found in a simple business operation. Here the inputs would comprise the money, materials, machinery, people, etc that are required for the business to operate; the processes are the way in which these are brought together and handled to ensure the provision of goods or services; and the outputs are the quality and quantity of goods or services the organisation seeks to provide. These inputs, processes, and outputs can also be spoken of as the causal, intervening, and output variables of an organisation. So Likert (1961:201) speaks of causal variables as being such things as organisational structures, organisational objectives, management and supervisory practices and behaviour, union contract, capital, investments, needs and desires of members of organisations etc. He sees the intervening variables as being such things as personality, perceptions, attitudes, motivational forces, behaviour, past experience, expectations, work group traditions, values and goals, and cognitive orientations such as information, my concept of my job or role, my concept of the roles of others to whom I relate etc. The end result variables Likert sees as being matters such as production, cost, waste, earnings, absence, turnover, union–company relations, grievances, stoppages, sales etc. It is these sorts of issues that are examined in the organisational x-ray.

We call it an x-ray because it performs exactly the same function as a medical x-ray. It does not place any value judgement on what is seen – it simply says here are the problem areas and here are the sound areas. When conducted properly such an x-ray looks at the organisation overall as well as each individual comprising the organisation so as to obtain a clear picture of relevant issues relating to their work performance and the overall achievement of organisational goals. To my mind this is an essential pre-requisite for effective human resource development and organisation development. It provides a base line from which ongoing interventions can start. (Long 1982, 1985, 1989).

Corporate planning

The old saying that 'if you don't know where you're going then any road will get you there' is true. Despite the truth of this saying, there is continual surprise at the number of organisations lacking clear goals and a sense of direction. If an organisation is to have an effective human resource development function it must ensure that any training provided works towards the achievement of organisational goals. This is impossible unless the organisation has defined those goals and enunciated them clearly to the human resource development people and general staff. Only when these goals are known can the human resource development unit and individuals know that the programmes they are proposing are in accord with the direction that the organisation wishes to go. In the event of an organisation not having its goals clearly defined and enunciated then no blame can be laid on the human resource development unit or any individual for failing to ensure that the correct form of training is provided. In the absence of clear planning the human resource development unit is totally justified in providing whatever programmes it deems to be appropriate regardless of whether or not such programmes are of direct benefit to the organisation.

One would think that this was self-evident yet experience indicates it is not. It is not uncommon for human resource development professionals to confess a lack of awareness of an organisation's corporate plan when I ask them for information prior to seeking to provide assistance. As recently as 1983 I was approached by the human resource development manager of a major oil company operating within Australia asking me to help him justify the existence of his department. The company was about to introduce staff cuts and he wanted to ensure that his department remained intact. Questioning quickly ascertained that he did not have access to corporate plans of the organisation and he was endeavouring to provide a service without knowing how his work was impacted upon by the rest of the organisation. This experience led me to survey other training professionals and, in far more instances than I believed possible, a similar story was found. I believe it to be essential that the human resource department be represented at the highest levels of an organisation if it is to function effectively and, as a result of involvement at the highest levels of an organisation, it must have access to the corporate plans so as to ensure that the work of the department is consistent with the goals of the organisation.

At this point it must be noted also that any human resource development policies propounded must be limited in the time-frame to which they apply. An organisation is a dynamic organism and, for that reason, human resource development policies and practices must be dynamic also. Many organisations seek to provide training for tomorrow using technology and techniques of the past and wonder why they are irrelevant in the present. In such instances the human resource development department may actually retard the organisation rather than promoting its achievement of goals. For this reason it is essential that an organisation looks at its present state and its goals at least annually. Once this is done then current human resource development policy can be propagated on a year-by-year basis.

It is not just the human resource development department that must be aware of the plans of an organisation. Obviously different levels of an organisation will have access to the corporate plan to differing extents but every person in an organisation should be aware of the strategic orientation of the organisation insofar as such plans impact on the individual's work. In fact Robinson and Pearce (1988:56) argue that where the strategic orientation of an organisation is known and where there is a consistency of and a high commitment to the strategy then an organisation has an average or above average likelihood of achieving its targets even with very low levels of planning sophistication. My own experience reinforces this viewpoint. I have found that when employees are totally aware of the short-term and long-term goals of the organisation together with the value system within which they operate then there is considerable innovation and enthusiasm for working as a team towards achieving these goals. In fact I find that providing such knowledge encourages people to seek out the learning required to ensure those goals are reached. This means that ensuring consistency of strategic orientation and a high commitment to the strategy is a very real aid to the development of a learner managed learning concept.

Corporate planning can be set out in the form of a hierarchy. One such hierarchy is illustrated at Figure 6.

The present level of knowledge and understanding of each employee

A mistake common to many organisations is to have a perception different from that of its people as to the current level of knowledge

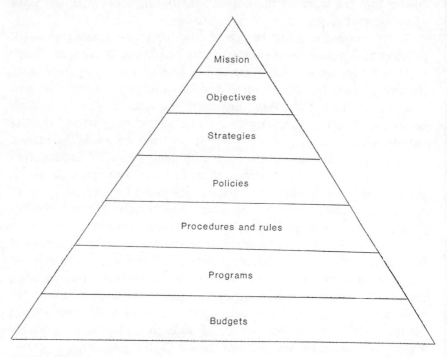

Figure 6   *A hierarchy of planning*

and understanding held by employees. Such an approach is totally incompatible with the concepts of adult learning (see Chapter 4). When people are sent on programmes because the organisation believes such programmes would be good for the individual (and/or the organisation) regardless of what that person may think or feel then the organisation is travelling a dangerous road. If the programme is significantly above the current level of knowledge and understanding of the individual then the person will feel inadequate and may reject totally the entire concept of training. If the programme is significantly below the current level of knowledge and understanding of the individual then they will consider the programme demeaning and, again, may reject totally the programme even if it has some relevance.

I was reminded of this during 1989 when, at the request of a client organisation, I was asked to conduct a leadership programme for their senior management. The training manager and I discussed the content that was required and, together, we came up with a programme that met the specifications set by the client. I was given a profile of the persons who would be attending and all preparations were made bearing in mind this profile and the requirements of the client. Seldom have I encountered such overt hostility as was the case when I walked into the training room on the first morning of the course. The attendees were significantly different from the profile provided; had been sent to the course against their wills – almost without exception they believed that training was applicable only for lower echelon personnel and most of them had not attended a training programme for periods of ten to fourteen years; and, in addition, various attendees objected to being on a course at the same time as other attendees from the same organisation. The course went downhill from here. Murphy's law, which states that when you feel something can't get any worse, it will, proved to be correct. The problem was a difference between the organisation's perception of the current level of knowledge and understanding of these employees and that held by themselves. In addition the failure of the organisation to brief participants as to the content and purpose of the programme and to insist that they attended without any such preparation exacerbated the situation.

The key to understanding the current level of knowledge and understanding of each employee is a thorough training needs analysis. By this I do not mean a training needs analysis in which the human resource development department discusses with managers and supervisors the needs of their subordinates for training and then prepares plans accordingly. I believe that if we are going to enable learner managed learning to be implemented then we must discuss with every person affected their own requirements for learning. This means full and frank discussions about their current level of performance with honest, open feedback as to deficiencies in behaviour and a confronting of differences between perceptions by supervisor and the supervised. Only when this is done is it possible for a meaningful training programme to be developed for any individual.

Organisational learning

Europe has been a leader in implementing approaches which approximate this model. Moloney (1982) in talking of her experience in France points out that the formal recognition of such an approach was recognised in 'The National Inter-Professional Agreement on Training' which was formalised between the Workers Union and the Employers Federations in July 1970. Under this agreement employers recognised the worker's right to occupational leave for training of their choice in normal work time. It also acknowledged the responsibility of the state to participate in training arrangements. This was formalised into 'the Act of 1971' in which employers were obliged to spend 1.1 per cent of their payroll on training and are required to provide proof that such expenditure was made. Accordingly, as Moloney says, when she was approached by a company she would study the company and the problems then make proposals. If the proposals called for a restructuring of part or all of the company they would propose also a training programme to accompany the changes and such training would be designed to meet the specific needs arising from the changes. In this regard the present state or position of the corporation was first ascertained together with its goals; the human resource development consultant/department next devised appropriate strategies to meet these goals and, starting from the present state of knowledge and experience of each learner, they provided the appropriate training. In July 1990 the Australian government introduced a similar concept (1 per cent of payroll over $200,000) and it will be interesting to monitor the impact this has on human resource development practices in Australia.

Stata (1989:64) suggest that organisational learning is the principal process by which management innovation occurs. He argues that the rate at which individuals and organisations learn may become the only sustainable competitive advantage especially in knowledge-intensive industries. (A point reinforced by Eisenhardt (1990) in her study of decision making and innovation). This begs the question of what is organisational learning and how does it differ from individual learning. I have argued already that individual learning is a process by which people gain new knowledge and insights with the result that they modify their behaviour and action. Stata argues that organisational learning entails new insights and modified behaviour but it differs from individual learning in that first, organisational learning occurs through shared insights, knowledge, and mental models. This means that organisations can learn only as fast as the slowest link learns. Change is blocked unless all of the major decision-makers learn together, come to share beliefs and goals and are committed to take the actions necessary for change. Second, learning builds on past knowledge and experience – that is, on memory. Organisational memory depends on institutional mechanisms (eg policies, strategies, explicit models) used to retain knowledge. Of course the memory of the individual is important, but relying exclusively on individuals risks losing hard-won lessons and experiences as people move from one job to another.

All of this endorses my earlier contention that training and education is too important for it to be left in the hands of a few select individuals. They may be highly trained and extremely competent. These individuals may be extremely highly motivated to pass on their knowledge and to facilitate change. I am not criticising human resource development professionals nor am I minimising the positive impact that they have had over the years. What I am saying is that, for too long, people in line management positions have abrogated their responsibility for the development of staff to these professionals with the result that the entire organisation has suffered. No matter how good the organisation may be and no matter how good the training and education supplied by human resource development professionals, unless that training and education is reinforced on the job and involves a very real partnership between the human resources department and line management then it is unlikely to have the maximum benefit possible.

Various countries have groups or bodies that operate as a 'think tank' or originator of ideas (concepts for discussion). One such of these is 'The Conference Board'. As far back as 1977 The Conference Board (Lusterman 1977) put out a paper in which they argued for industry to see itself as part of the nation's educational system along with colleges, universities, technical institutes, and other schools. Rather than seeing itself as being in competition with the formal educational system the training and education provided within a corporate context should be complimentary to the formal educational systems. I suggest that for this to have maximum benefit, both within the corporate context and the educational system, learner managed learning must be encouraged in both areas.

Nadler (1982) suggests that the provision of education and training within a corporate context involves distinct steps which start and end with identifying the needs of the organisation. The provision of training is the penultimate step in the series and it occurs only after careful attention has been paid to the present state or position of the corporation, its corporate goals, and the present level of knowledge and understanding of each employee. Nadler shows how one must start by identifying the needs of the organisation; next specify job performance; then identify learner needs. It is only after this is done that it becomes possible to determine objectives, to build a curriculum, and to select instructional strategies. Failure to follow these steps leads to frustration in all areas of the organisation and, ultimately, to the denigration of training and education within the corporate context. If, however, these steps are followed then it becomes possible to co-ordinate all learning with the corporate goals and strategic plans. It ensures that all learning starts from the present knowledge/competency of the learner and, if done properly, it ensures that all learning is programmed to suit the rate of assimilation of the knowledge of the learner. In other words it encourages learner managed learning. This enables us also to encourage the innovative learning advocated by the Club of Rome Report and referred to in Chapter 1.

When Eric moved from the university to a consulting organisation he expected respect because of his academic background. What he found was that most business executives are critical of the performance of the nation's schools and colleges in preparing people for work. He encountered criticism because of the low standard in reading, writing, and arithmetic employers encountered amongst younger employees. He discovered that many executives believe that our teacher training organisations would do well to copy industry in its growing emphasis on student participation and the blending of classroom study with programmed self-study and planned problem solving experience. He found that clients were results-oriented and demanded that performance standards be set and met for every assignment. The consultancy to which he went placed heavy importance on adequate preparation for every training programme and seldom allowed a lecture to be read. This meant that he could no longer prepare a series of lectures and present those over a protracted period. Instead he had to re-prepare for every presentation. He had assumed that training within industry – ie learning in a corporate context – would be very similar to teaching in a university environment. In his instance he found that this was not the case and this had near devastating results in the short term for his professional self-esteem. In the long-term Eric was successful at making the transition. But for this to happen his paradigm required changing.

10 Learner Managed Learning and the Human Resource Development Professional

Case study: *Words or deeds?*

In January 1985 Fiona took up the appointment of Manager for Training Services within a major Australian organisation providing training and education to the corporate sector. For the twenty years immediately preceding this appointment Fiona had been involved in providing training services either as a company trainer or as a consultant. She was recognised as a leading professional within the human resource development community and she had been involved in the design of key government programmes designed to train trainers within industry.

Fiona was a strong proponent of the principles of adult learning and sought to encourage self-direction in learning wherever possible.

The organisation she joined had been in existence for some forty years and had moved from being a volunteer operation offering training on an *ad hoc* basis to a national organisation employing some 150 people on a full-time basis and a further 300 on a part-time basis. Their curriculum encompassed basic skills training through to upper middle-management level training. It enjoyed an enviable reputation in the community and had little or no trouble attracting part-time faculty to augment the full-time members involved in providing training and education.

Almost the first task performed by Fiona was an examination of the standards of education and training provided by the full-time and part-time faculty. She examined appraisals completed by course participants; she read the curriculum vitaes of every trainer; she sat in on training and educational courses; and she met with every faculty member (both full-time and part-time) in order to discuss their perceived performance and to ascertain areas in which they sought assistance. She was appalled with what she found. A significant proportion of the faculty had experience but no training as trainers or educators and virtually none of the faculty had attended any professional development programme within the previous five years. Most of the teaching styles were primarily didactic with little or no attention being paid to the principles of adult learning.

As a first step to deal with this Fiona developed a series of evening workshops to cover key issues relating to adult education. These were conducted once a month and were designed as partly a social gathering and partly a learning experience.

In designing these programmes Fiona went to her chief executive to ensure full acquaintance with the strategic orientation of the organisation. She was made privy to the five year corporate plan and she met with each of the course directors to ascertain their concerns and needs.

When she was organising the first of these programmes Fiona approached both the CEO and her own immediate manager with the request that they be present at each function and that they endorse her actions by opening and closing each session as well as stressing the importance for professional development. The first session was well attended by faculty members but neither Fiona's manager nor the CEO appeared. Both had said they would endeavour to be present. When Fiona met with them the following day apologies were profuse but 'other more important matters' had arisen and they were unable to be present. Both said they would endeavour to be present at the next workshop. Despite pressure and pleadings from Fiona no firm commitment was given.

This pattern occurred with the second and third workshops and Fiona noticed a significant drop in attendance over the period. When she remonstrated with her superiors they countered her protestations with the statement 'we are here to teach management, not to practise it'. The workshops fizzled to a stop by year's end.

Within two years Fiona had ceased to try to be a human resource development professional within this culture and was employed elsewhere.

Corporate culture and values

For most people learner managed learning usually takes place in association with various kinds of helpers facilitators, peers, etc. For this reason some organisations argue that, because they conduct an intensive training needs analysis which asks individuals in the organisation to identify needs, it follows that they are involved in learner managed learning. This is not necessarily the case. Every organisation has its own values and culture. In the majority of organisations these values and culture conform to the traditional paradigm in which learning primarily depends on the input of a teacher or trainer. In this situation, even if there has been input from the individual as to the learning required, the experience may not really be learner managed learning. Very often the conducting of a training needs analysis and discussion with participants (including input from them as to the programmes required) is a public relations exercise in obtaining compliance by participants. The needs of the learner may be taken into account and, in many instances, such tools as programmed learning, audio cassette packages, video packages, personal computer packages, current management texts, computer-based learning, and interactive video instruction are utilised yet, when the process is analysed, the approach is far from learner managed learning. Particularly is this the case when organisations are seeking a 'quick fix' because they do not wish to deal with the underlying cause of any particular problem or issue.

In 1986 at the International Training of Trainers Programme conducted by the University of Southern California's School of Public Administration I suggested that effective human resource development required interaction between the organisation, the human resource department, and the individual receiving training. Again, such interaction should be self-evident but, in practice although not in theory, the interaction between these three does not always occur.

The organisation

If we consider the interaction between organisation, human resource development department and individual as a triangle then the base of the triangle is the organisation itself. The organisation is the main environmental factor in which human resource development professionals operate.

Because of this pivotal environmental role the organisation has key responsibilities if human resource development is to be effective. First the organisation must have a real commitment to the whole concept of human resource development. This commitment is not just a statement in some document of mission or philosophy but it is a commitment of sufficient strength to ensure that human resource development receives a high priority at all levels of the organisation. Accordingly once this commitment is made, the organisation will make and propagate the human resource development policies and will set the parameters in which human resource development is to be conducted. They will follow this by providing the finance required and by ensuring that adequate time is made available for both the human resource development department and individuals to fulfil their part in people development. In addition to this they will show their commitment to human resource development by ensuring a high profile from senior management in appropriate courses and programmes. This participation will mean such things as having a senior executive (at least very close to the chief executive officer if the chief executive officer cannot attend) attend either the opening or the closing of any programme or both. They will ensure also that even senior executives are seen to have their own human resource development programme and to be implementing it. The final part of organisational involvement is to ensure that adequate support is given to the human resource development department and to individuals so that learning can be implemented and changes can be made. In other words they will ensure that learning is not something divorced from the work situation but that people actually can use that which has been provided and to which they have committed themselves.

An illustration of this is found in the different approaches taken by successive chief executive officers of an electricity supply authority. In 1986 I conducted a series of training programmes that were attended by four senior members of this particular organisation. As a result of this I was invited to meet with their chief executive officer and, a little later, to conduct a further training programme for him and his direct reports. This led to my working with the training manager to devise and develop a training programme for their supervisory and lower level management staff. This programme went well but there was no involvement by senior management at opening or closing the programmes and, in many instances, people complained that their management should be attending these sessions.

In 1987 this chief executive officer retired and he was replaced by one of the four people who had attended the initial series of programmes. By the end of 1988 the new man was ready to move and, at the start of 1989, he requested me to develop a programme for the very first line supervisory personnel – the gangers and leading hands. The approach taken was to meet with future course participants to ascertain their real needs and to obtain an indication of their current levels of knowledge and understanding. This data gathering session proved potentially explosive as the leading hands and gangers listed their grievances and concerns as well as ways that they could see for saving the authority money and operating more effectively.

The data gathering sessions were followed by feedback to the same groups at which we reported on the findings and checked that we were fairly representing their views. These feedback sessions were attended by the new chief executive officer. No matter how early the sessions started or how distant they were from his office or home he was present and listened carefully to what was said. Where a decision could be made immediately and action taken he made that decision and the impact on morale was tremendous. For the first time the leading hands and gangers had face-to-face contact with their chief executive officer under circumstances in which they could openly voice their concerns and cares and get frank, honest responses from him. These sessions were followed by a training programme designed to improve the people-skills of leading hands and supervisors in their training role of working with their subordinates. Again the CEO attended at least one session of each of these programmes no matter what personal inconvenience to himself. In addition he insisted that, on the third day of each programme, at least one other senior manager was also present.

This authority has not yet fully incorporated aspects of adult learning and the second phase is to commence in 1990. However, the evidence to date is quite clear that people throughout the organisation are aware of the organisation's commitment to training and there is no doubt in anyone's mind that training provided must be implemented. The chief executive officer himself reports a substantial improvement in performance throughout the organisation simply as a result of the morale boost that has occurred because, for the first time, there is total consistency between what is said about commitment to training and what is shown by the chief executive officer and his direct reports.

The human resource development department

From the very nature of this department it must follow that there is a commitment to human resource development.

Included in the responsibility of the human resource development department is the administering of the corporate policy regarding human resource development. In conjunction with this there will be a variety of functions they need to perform. Included in these functions are:

- The conducting of training needs analyses;
- Maintaining adequate training records;
- Statutory compliance;
- Developing, conducting, and/or co-ordinating the entire human resource development function;
- Evaluating training programmes and their effect on participants;
- Gathering data associated with human resource development in general and the issues relevant to the company in particular;
- Ensuring a link between the training situation and the practical work situation;
- Implementing the training plan;
- Acting as a resource centre to the individuals and company as a whole;
- Acting as a catalyst for all human resource development functions;
- Ensuring adequate follow-up is done on all human resource development activities.

This is significantly more complex than that which was done by a simple, earlier style, training function. In this approach it is quite possible that those in the human resource development area may never conduct training programmes. Their role may be far more that of finding appropriate sources for training and co-ordinating training rather than doing up-front presentations.

My experience shows that, in most organisations, the human resource development department tends to conduct numbers of courses with attendance by groups of people with similar needs. Very often these will be technically oriented and, in general, will be designed to assist people to do their present job more effectively or to prepare people for positions into which they are about to move. Executive and line management (often endorsed by human resource development practitioners) seem to believe that unless a human resource development practitioner is actively involved in hands-on training they are not fulfilling the role for which they are paid.

For learner managed learning to become operative it is essential that there be a change in mind-set regarding the human resource development department. In a learner managed learning concept a significant proportion of the human resource development department's time will be spent in acting as a resource centre and a catalyst rather than being involved in 'hands-on training'. As discussed in Chapter 3, unless the environment in which the human resource development professional is operating becomes conducive to a change in paradigm then it is unlikely that learner managed learning can be implemented. Many managers and organisations feel threatened by the learner managed learning approach and, for that reason, attempts will be made to dress-up the traditional paradigm as learner managed learning. This is a pressure that must be resisted by human resource development professionals who are genuinely interested in implementing learner managed learning and reaping the benefits that are possible from this.

Again consider an example. In the period until mid-1988 the Australian operations of a major multinational organisation had enjoyed a number of years stability as regards its chief executive officer. During this time the organisation consolidated its Australian head office in the heart of Sydney and saw the human resource development department as being largely an internal consultancy acting as a resource to the various operating units. The change in chief executive officer coincided with adverse economic conditions within Australia and general turmoil in the key industries with which this organisation was involved. By late 1989 the company had its third chief executive officer in two years and the head office function had been disbanded totally. The human resource development department was now the training function for one of the operating companies and the move had been made back to the human resource development professionals being heavily involved in hands-on training. By early 1990 the situation had arisen in which the human resource development department had no time available for evaluation of the training provided and were unable to perform virtually any other function than that of providing hands-on training. At a time when the organisation needed to maximise its return on every training dollar expended it had actually moved into a phase in which there existed a very high risk that training dollars would be wasted. Instead of continuing the previous move towards the new paradigm of cost-effective learner managed learning, when the crisis came the organisation reverted to a paradigm which their own experience had previously told them was inappropriate if the organisation was to grow, develop, and to be increasingly effective. A direct result of this was that key human resource development professionals sought job opportunities elsewhere rather than continue along a path that, in the long term, had been proven to have detrimental effects on the organisation.

The individual

It would be nice to assume that individuals attending training pro-grammes were committed to the concept of learning. Unfortunately this is not necessarily the case. In the long-term, if human resource development is to be of benefit, it is essential that the trainee be committed to the concept of training in general as well as recognising the value of any particular programme for him or her when attending it. Accordingly, for this interaction to be effective, the individual needs to have a commitment to lifelong learning in general and especially to its application to themselves. Once this commitment is made then the person is ready to move to the point of taking responsibility for their own learning. It is important to note that they are taking responsibility for their own learning. We are not talking here of learning that is superimposed upon them by the organisation or the human resource development department. In learner managed learning the individual identifies particular needs that they have; they identify the goals to be reached; and they seek opportunities for learning and development. In this way they are responsible for the learning that they undertake.

For this to be effective it is important that individuals are aware of the overall human resource development policies and their application to themselves. They must respect these policies and seek to undertake their training within the framework of those policies.

Obviously this is different from what occurs in the majority of cases. In many organisations all training decisions are made by line managers who, often under pressure from the human resource development department, send their subordinates on training courses whether or not such a course is really appropriate and, almost always, without adequate briefing of the trainee prior to attending the course. In other instances the human resource development department circulates a shopping list of training courses and invites people to nominate for them. Although basically a good concept, often this approach is abused by people seeing such courses as an escape from the workfront rather than being an opportunity for growth and development.

Learner managed learning is results oriented. Because of this the individual must be committed to the goals that are set. This requires that a mechanism be set up to monitor progress – mutually agreed upon – towards these goals and overall results. In this way the individual becomes responsible for their own progress and answers both to the human resource development department and to the organisation as a whole for the attainment of agreed results.

Consider the case of Pauline.

Pauline is in her late 40s. In her early 20s she had met an Australian man on holiday in England and by the late 1960s they had married and were living in Sydney. When Pauline was in her early 30s and, with three young children, her husband was killed in an accident and, as he was uninsured, Pauline shouldered the total responsibility for supporting her family. She returned to clerical work and, over the succeeding ten years, developed a wide range of clerical and secretarial capabilities. During this period she worked primarily in small organisations. In 1986 Pauline joined a major national organisation as administrative assistant to a senior executive. This organisation claimed to provide opportunities for all employees to experience growth and development by undergoing any of the training programmes offered. As is often the case there was a significant difference between theory and fact but, by applying considerable pressure, Pauline was allowed to attend one work related training programme in the period to December 1987.

As a result of her frustration with the difference between theory and fact (but being totally committed to her own development), Pauline decided to seek personal development in outside organisations. Pauline believed that, with appropriate opportunities, she could utilise the vast experience she had gained since her husband's death by assisting small businesses in their overall administration. At the start of 1988 she was accepted for a graduate diploma programme offered by one of Sydney's universities and arranged her study programme in such a way as to ensure all lectures and tutorials were held during evenings and weekends.

Pauline's manager saw such an approach as being within the policy framework of the organisation and encouraged her in this regard. Her opinion was that, when these additional qualifications were obtained, Pauline would be of even more value to the organisation and she took active steps to ensure Pauline had opportunity of attending other training programmes offered by the company. This manager left the organisation at the end of 1988 and Pauline's new manager subscribed to the fact rather than the theory of the organisation's training policies. Suddenly Pauline found herself under pressure to work evenings and weekends with the result that her studies suffered. Appeals to the human resource development manager brought no positive response and, by mid-1989, Pauline had to choose between achieving the results she had set for herself or experiencing continued frustration within her employment. As at January 1990 Pauline is running a very successful operation providing administrative support and assistance to small business and she is well on her way to graduating at the end of the year.

What Fiona encountered was a classic example of the difference between fact and theory. In theory Fiona's employer agreed on the balance of organisation, human resource development department and individual. In accord with this theory they gave lip-service to the role of the organisation to endorse and support the development of their people. In fact the chief executive officer and Fiona's manager both took the approach that it was up to those in training to handle all aspects of training and there was no line or corporate responsibility involved. In the case of Fiona's employer this approach had resulted in an annual turnover of in excess of 40 per cent amongst senior executives. Only the chief executive officer, Fiona's boss, and two others out of fifteen executives had served with the organisation for three or more years.

11 Learner Managed Learning within the Educational Context

Case study: *Better late than never!*

While at secondary school, Julie had a disappointing career. Although undoubtedly bright she exhibited an inability to pass examinations and, by the end of her third year, had decided to drop out. She obtained work as a clerk and, by age 22, was handling all credit enquiries for the local branch of a home furnishing chain.

She had always liked dealing with children and, apart from contact with her younger siblings, she had been involved in the scouting movement as a leader. In 1967 the opportunity arose for her to move into child care work and, as a result of this, she was encouraged to commence studying for a certificate in child care. She obtained this certificate and, realising that she did have the ability to undertake formal education, she again tried for and obtained her matriculation. At age 33 she commenced her training as a teacher and she has now experienced some ten years in the teaching profession and is highly respected by her peers and students as well as by her employers. Looking back she often expresses concern about the way in which her initial three years of secondary education almost prevented her from fulfilling her dream of teaching.

The measurement of excellence

Kabuga (1977:25) says:

It appears to me that people who remember most may not necessarily be the ones who think more. While remembering is a backward-looking activity, thinking is a future one, and it is my conviction that any dynamic society needs more of such future-looking citizens. It is because pedagogy does nothing other than develop the memory of the learner that it is outmoded, either as a tool for the education of children or adults.

As I said in Chapter 1, the traditional paradigm of learning has been questioned for some time. We have recognised the shortcomings of the pedagogical approach yet for reasons of comfort, security, and familiarity we have sought to modify the existing paradigm rather than replace it. Accordingly we have looked at different forms of pedagogy such as programmed instruction, computer-based training, interactive video instruction and the like, rather than move towards a new approach. Fortunately this is now changing. The last ten years have seen a significant increase in the number of colleges and universities which use some form of learner managed learning and who seek to use an andragogical rather than a pedagogical approach to the entire learning process.

If we consider learning in terms of a normal business or manufacturing equation then it has three components. An input, a process, and an output. Diagrammatically we can show this as:

$$I \rightarrow P \rightarrow O$$

Originally learning was geared towards particular outputs. Socrates on a stoa in Athens sought, by means of questions, to encourage his pupils to greater understanding of what they were saying and the overall mysteries of life. The input was himself and his students; the process was the Socratic dialogue; the output was an increase in understanding by both parties. During the twentieth century particularly we have changed the emphasis. With our concentration upon the attaining of academic qualifications we have said that the output is to be the attaining of a degree or other qualification. The inputs and the processes then become totally geared towards that end. We see this in, for example, the requirement for standardised test results to be at a particular level before a person is allowed to embark upon a particular course of study. So, in our secondary education system, we gear the entire process towards assisting young people to obtain the scores that will enable them to take up the academic pursuit of their choice. In order to do this we make judgements as to the relative difficulty between particular courses so that we can scale raw scores in such a way that will maximise the chances of the desired output being obtained – ie obtaining academic excellence as measured by standardised test scores and the right of admission to prestige universities.

That such an approach is fraught with danger is self-evident. Not infrequently we encounter instances of cheating, collusion, and, in extreme cases, teenage suicides by people for whom the pressure of providing such output becomes too much.

It is important to make one thing very clear. I am not denigrating academic excellence. What I am querying is the means by which we measure academic excellence and the process by which we seek to attain it. Currently we tend to measure academic excellence in terms of examination results rather than demonstrated competency to do the work. It is this that has given rise to the popular joke of 'we all know what BS is, MS is more of the same, while a PhD is simply all that piled higher and deeper'. Obviously this joke is an over-statement but, like many jokes, it contains an element of truth. Consider the following example.

In 1979 I was approached by a major mining company to develop a programme for their graduate entrants. This company had a policy of recruiting graduates in their early twenties and immediately placing them into supervisory positions over people who had been with the company for two, three, four or more years. The graduate, by dint of his or her having completed a degree, was presumed to have more knowledge than the person who had been doing the work for some significant time. Not surprisingly the company was experiencing dissatisfaction among its longer-term non-graduate employees and, simultaneously, was experiencing an extremely high level of turnover among the graduates who found that nothing in their academic work had prepared them for the responsibility of obtaining results through other people. Despite their knowledge from an academic perspective these young graduates lacked experience in applying this knowledge and they were being placed in the untenable position of being expected to supervise the quality and quantity of output of people whose only shortcoming was that they did not have a piece of paper proclaiming them as 'being qualified'. Under such circumstances it was not surprising that supervisors were held in low regard; the overall quality of supervision was poor; and there was a high turnover among such appointees.

In Chapter 7 I quoted Jackson and Prosser (1986) and Bock (1986), who argue for a competency-based assessment in education. It is important to note that no matter how much the educational assessment for graduates in accounting, engineering, business studies, or any other discipline may be competency-based, it is extremely unlikely that any such formal academic programme would be able to prepare graduates for a role such as this mining company expected them to fulfil. My point here is that a competency-based assessment would have better equipped these graduates for transition to the workforce. My criticism is of the company for putting these young graduates into such an untenable position.

The learner-centred approach

Rogers (1961) argues that for individual growth in terms of developing a sense of individual identity (ie 'becoming a person') people must:

- Become more aware of reality as it exists outside of themselves instead of perceiving it in preconceived categories.
- Develop a more immediate awareness of unsatisfying consequences so as to enable a quicker correction of choices which are an error.
- Develop an increasing locus of evaluation and control within themselves.

Rogers argues that as this occurs an individual develops the ability to assimilate the evidence of a new situation as it is rather than distorting it to fit a pattern which is already held. This increasing ability to be open to experience makes a person more realistic in dealing with new people, new situations, and new problems. Obviously it also encourages self-reliance and an honest appraisal of one's strengths and weaknesses so as to enable a balanced approach to life. This is totally consistent with the hermeneutic view of man (Sullivan 1986) that was discussed in Chapter 7. Rogers argues that central to all of this is an awareness '. . . that it rests within himself to choose; that the only question that matters is "am I living in a way which is deeply satisfying to me, and which truly expresses me?"'

Rogers approaches the issue from the perspective of psychotherapy and, of course, this approach was central to his therapeutic work. However, he is adamant that, in the educational arena, it is the student-centred or learner-centred approach that, ultimately, will have most benefit for organisations and individuals. He sees this as being a crucial part of their obtaining overall psychological wholeness. In fact he goes on to say (page 280) that, as a result of realising identity as a person the following sorts of changes occur:

- the person comes to see himself differently
- he accepts himself and his feelings more fully
- he becomes more self-confident and more self-directing
- he becomes more the person he would like to be
- he becomes more flexible, less rigid, in his perception
- he adopts more realistic goals for himself
- he behaves in a more mature fashion
- he changes his maladjustive behaviours, even such a long-established one as chronic alcoholism
- he becomes more acceptant of others
- he becomes more open to the evidence, both what is going on

outside of himself, and to what is going on inside himself
• he changes in his basic characteristics, in constructive ways

A number of these relate specifically to self-identity in a counselling situation, but many of them are equally true for the overall learner managed learning approach. The emphasis in learner managed learning is on self-reliance and self-actualisation. People obtain the ability to tap increasing depths of potential within themselves and, by so doing, experience significant personal growth and learning. In conjunction with this, Rogers' comment on significant learning must be noted. Again, on page 280, he says:

> By significant learning I mean learning which is more than an accumulation of facts. It is learning which makes a difference – in the individual's behaviour, in the course of action he chooses in the future, in his attitudes and his personality. It is a pervasive learning which is not just an accretion of knowledge, but which inter-penetrates with every portion of his existence.

Obviously this involves both the maintenance and innovative learning that is advocated in the Club of Rome Report (Botkin, Elmadjra, and Malitza (1989)) referred to in Chapter 1. Surely such learning ought to be the goal of our educational institutions and all aspects of the formal learning process. I recognise that, in theory, this is what formal education is all about. I suggest that, in practice, there is a significant gap between what is intended and what occurs.

My key point here is that, as set out in Chapter 10, if a person really wants to learn, if the learning experience is tailored to that person, and if they are put into an environment in which learning is encouraged, then significant growth can and will occur with the result that previously low achievers can experience increasing degrees of self-actualisation. In this regard it is essential that our formal educational processes encourage a forward-looking approach rather than simply the accretion of historical and other data. Education should not be merely an intellectual exercise but rather something that is applicable in every area of life. It may start in one small segment of an individual's life but, if nourished, it will develop and it has the potential to impact positively on every aspect of that person. Accordingly we should be encouraging individuals to strive for such an approach whether we are talking about academia, the workplace, sporting activities, or any other aspect of life experience.

From an academic point of view there is sometimes criticism of self-directed or learner centred learning because, as Rogers (1961:277) says:

> ... (b) We would do away with examinations. They measure only the inconsequential type of learning.

(c) The implication would be that we would do away with the grades and credits for the same reason.

(d) We would do away with Degrees as a measure of competence partly for the same reason. Another reason is that a degree marks an end or a conclusion of something, and a learner is only interested in the continuing process of learning.

If learner managed learning advocated such an approach to the total exclusion of professional standards and the denigrating of academic excellence then one could make a very strong argument that it was not applicable in the formal educational arena. But, as Rogers goes on to say (page 290):

> In such an education, the requirements for many life situations would be part of the resources the teacher provides. The teacher would have available the knowledge that he cannot enter engineering school without so much math; that he cannot get a job in corporation 'x' unless he has a college Diploma; that he cannot become a psychologist without doing independent doctoral research; that he cannot be a doctor without knowledge of chemistry; that he cannot even drive a car without passing an examination on rules of the road. These requirements are set, not by the teacher, but by life. The teacher is there to provide the resources which the student can use to learn so as to be able to meet these tests

In other words learner managed learning is not advocating that we discard or in any way denigrate professional standards and requirements. Learner managed learning recognises and totally accepts that professional standards must be set and maintained and that persons wishing to enter professions must comply with these standards. The difference between learner managed learning and the traditional approach to standards is that, in the traditional approach, there can be a tendency for an individual to see the qualification as an end in itself. There are people who obtain their qualification and give the impression that, having reached this goal, they do not need to upgrade their knowledge or skills. Such an attitude is actively discouraged by most professions and many of them have introduced their 'professional year' requirements which make it obligatory for a person wishing to maintain professional status and accreditation within their discipline to attend a certain number of professional year activities. The learner managed learning approach seeks to encourage an attitude in which such professional year activities are actively sought and welcomed rather than being seen as an imposition. Because the self-directed learner has taken responsibility for reaching professional standards and for continuing in lifelong learning, there is a tendency to welcome professional year activities as a means of furthering lifelong learning. Indeed, experience seems to indicate that the lifelong learner continues to make contracts with himself or herself to ensure that further learning does occur after qualifications have been obtained (this issue of contracts or agreements will be discussed in Chapter 12). If this learning is widespread it would appear that the learner managed learning paradigm should be welcomed and encouraged by any professional body seeking to propagate and maintain the highest standards of ability and performance by their members.

The question arises as to how one teaches quantitative disciplines such as engineering, physics, chemistry, computer science, accountancy, geology, etc in a self-directed approach. It is relatively easy to accept that qualitative areas such as interpersonal relationships, personal growth, and the like can be taught in a non-directive fashion. Is the same true of these quantitative subjects? I believe that the answer is 'yes'. The way in which this can be done takes us back to Knowles' model as to the mix between pedagogy and andragogy. This is discussed in Chapter 4. Knowles argues that we should seek to introduce some aspects of andragogical principles right from the earliest days so that we can encourage an individual to become self-reliant (in Rogers' terms, to promote growth in their becoming a person and, in Maslow's terms, to encourage growth motivation). As already discussed in Chapter 4 there is no conflict between Knowles and Rogers in this regard. If we are to introduce a balance between andragogy and pedagogy it is imperative that we treat each learner as an individual in their own right. This requires a very learner-centred approach to education as some people will move more rapidly than others into taking responsibility for their own learning experience. The goal, however, is, during the formal educational period of primary and secondary schooling, to encourage the growth in an andragogical approach by all students so that when they move on to post-secondary education they have an understanding of goal setting, contracting for learning, and goal achievement. In this approach, once the learner reaches the post-secondary stage, they would contract to obtain from the professor those mandatory requirements for them to enter a profession and they would then take responsibility for designing a learning programme that ensured these requirements would be met. In this regard the post-secondary education would have available resources such as lectures, libraries, video-based learning, and all other appropriate resources by which the learner could obtain the requisite knowledge. The means of assessing the knowledge obtained would continue to be set by the professional accrediting organisation or body and the student would choose to meet these requirements.

The difference between this approach and that which is presently used lies in the emphasis being made. In our traditional approach the university system uses a standardised test score result to determine which students shall have the right of entry on which courses. It then, generally in association with the appropriate professional bodies, determines the educational programme to be undergone both in terms of content and order of study, and confronts the student with a 'take it or leave it' approach. Progress through the course is then measured by means of exam results with the emphasis being on one's ability to remember facts and historical data rather than on the exhibition of competencies within that field. It is made mandatory for students wishing to obtain credits to attend a certain number of lectures and/or tutorials as well as demonstrating this knowledge in the formal assessment. If we moved to a self-directed mode then the emphasis would be on the learner providing evidence of having obtained the knowledge while the means by which that knowledge is attained would be left to the discretion of the learner with a faculty member acting as a facilitator in that individual's learning process. Even the assessments would be based more on the demonstration of competency rather than on the ability to regurgitate data.

That this creates practical difficulties for traditional schools is obvious. In part this is seen by Jackson and Prosser (1986) as discussed in Chapter 7. In the self-directed approach there is no guarantee that students would be attending any lecture or tutorial. The onus on the professor would move from being a disseminator of knowledge through to being a facilitator in the learning process and acting as a resource on a one-to-one or one-to-group basis with the learners. It creates difficulties in determining the number of students who would be attending any particular assessment centre for evaluation of their knowledge. Such evaluations may need to be done more frequently and for smaller groups. This, in turn, will place increasing demands on all staff. However, it would enable those learning at a rapid pace to proceed through their learning programmes in a shorter period than their slower peers. It would mean that some people may complete their professional qualifications a year or more ahead of the traditional time-spans.

These issues indicate some of the very real problems associated with a learner managed learning approach in the formal educational system. (These problems will be elaborated further in Chapter 13). But these problems are not insurmountable. If there is a belief that learner managed learning really does benefit the individual, the profession, and society then difficulties will be faced and ways of implementing learner managed learning will be found. Unfortunately, though, the experience Rogers had in 1952 (Rogers 1961:274) still tends to be echoed today. When Rogers, at a conference organised by Harvard University, gave his personal thoughts on teaching and learning, he recounts his experience as:

I was hoping for a response, but I did not expect the tumult that followed. Feeling ran high. It seemed I was threatening their jobs, I was obviously saying things I didn't mean, etc, etc.

Such avoidance behaviour can, in the long term, only be detrimental to the individual, professions, and society at large.

Obviously where I have been talking in terms of professions there is a direct correlation with the obtaining of formal academic qualifications through established colleges and universities. From my experience, it appears as though the current situation with the majority of academic institutions whether in Australia, the United States, Canada, the United Kingdom, or other places, is an emphasis on a traditional rather than a self-directed approach. These institutions tend to encourage students to absorb knowledge rather than encouraging learners to take an active part in seeking the knowledge they require and accepting responsibility for their learning process. This approach is changing and, from my own experience, institutions such as the School of Public Administration at the University of Southern California, Los Angeles, the Union Institute in Cincinnati, Brunel University of West London, the University of Technology, New South Wales, and Macquarie University in New South Wales, are amongst those that are implementing aspects of learner managed learning in their programmes.

This is not occurring without some cost and pain. Macquarie University have experienced criticism of their Law Faculty because, rather than taking a traditional approach to teaching law, they used a more innovative learning approach which emphasised the philosophy on which the law is based rather than a rote learning of various cases and judicial decisions. In 1989 the issue reached the levels of national attention with claims and counter-claims being made against the department and its academic staff. I suspect that many of those on the faculty of the Macquarie University Law School would argue that Rogers' experience at Harvard was separated only by some thirty years from their own experience.

One of the exciting things I have experienced in many traditional schools is a willingness of recent days to experiment with a learner managed learning approach. In 1986 I was approached by Drexel University in Philadelphia as to the possibility of visiting with them during 1987. In January 1987 I visited the school to present two lectures in which I outlined my philosophy of teaching. Despite the fact that, so far as I could ascertain, Drexel was (and probably still is) a very traditional school my appointment to the Visiting Faculty was confirmed and I commenced teaching there in April 1987. I was given total discretion as to the way in which I covered the material with my classes on organisation behaviour and, even though my approach probably created some difficulties for other members of the Faculty, the response from the head of the department was positive and they have invited me back. I have not yet seen evidence that any department within Drexel University is moving totally to a learner managed learning approach but I do see a willingness within the university to examine inputs, processes, and outputs with the intention that students should be encouraged to undertake learning rather than education *per se*.

This willingness at least to investigate learner managed learning has been assisted in no small part by the work of people such as Knowles (1970, 1975, 1984), Kolb and Boyatsis (1984), Kolb and Fry (1975), Kolb, Rubin and McIntyre (1984), Nadler (1980, 1982), Nadler and Wiggs (1986) Rogers (1961, 1970), Zemke (1981) and others. Their work has led to people such as Tenenbaum (1961:311) who, writing of his first movements into a learner managed learning mode within a university setting writes:

> It is true that since I was influenced by the Kilpatrick methodology I've always welcomed the widest discussion, but I now know, I still wanted and expected students to know the text and the lecture material set out for them. Even worse, I now know that although I welcomed discussion, I wanted, above all things, that, after all was said and done, the final conclusions of the task to come out according to my way of thinking. Hence none of the discussions were real discussions, in the sense that it was open and free and enquiring; none of the questions were real questions, in the sense that they sought to evoke thinking; all of them were loaded, in the sense that I had pretty definite convictions about what I thought were good answers and at times right answers. Hence, I came to the class with subject matter and my students were really instruments by which situations were manipulated to produce the inclusion of what I regarded as desirable subject matter.
>
> In this last course, I didn't have the courage to discard all subject matter, but this time I really listened to my students; I gave them understanding and sympathy. Although I would spend hours and hours preparing for each session, I found that not once did I refer to a note from the voluminous material with which I entered the room. I allowed students free reign, not holding anyone down to any set course, and I permitted the widest diversion; and I followed wherever the students led. . . .
>
> I cannot say I followed you all the way Dr. Rogers, since I would express opinions and at times, unfortunately, lecture; and that I believe is bad, since students, once authoritative opinions are expressed, tend not to think, but to try to guess what is in the instructors head and provide him with what he might like, so as to find favour in his eyes.

My experience (and from discussions with other people involved in learner managed learning processes – a common experience) is that our first forays into learner managed learning were not dissimilar from those experienced by Tenenbaum. It was scary. It challenged everything that we had done in the past and the way in which we had ourselves received much of our education. But, in the long term, it was infinitely more rewarding and resulted in a growth experience for both professor and class.

Of course it is not just the professor who experiences shock. I have watched the look of surprise and consternation that comes over people's faces when people such as David Kolb or Ron Fry of Case Western University start a programme with middle managers. I have seen the total unbelief come across faces of my own students, and, especially at Drexel University, found a very real unwillingness to accept that I was genuine in taking this non-traditional approach. But, as both parties have become committed to the concept and have shared the pains and the joys of the learner managed learning experience, it has become a valuable growth experience for everyone involved.

This was Julie's experience. When, in 1967, we first met she had just decided to accept the position in child care and, although knowing that she wanted to work with children, she was apprehensive about her ability to cope with the academic demands. She had no doubt whatsoever about her practical ability – it was her past educational experience that created the doubts. With her successes grew also her confidence. It took time, but as she took increasing responsibility for her own growth and development she was able to overcome problems associated with being a mature-age student, bringing up a young family as a solo parent, and establishing a career.

12 Learning Agreements

Case study: *Please confirm in writing*

Martin was convinced that learner managed learning was for him. He lived in New York and he had undergraduate and graduate degrees from very well-known universities. When I first met him he had just enrolled on a doctoral programme through the learner managed learning methodology. He was very intelligent. He grasped the concepts quickly and he exhibited rapid growth in terms of the ability continuum of implementing the learner managed learning programme. However, Martin had a problem. He believed that a verbal commitment to learner managed learning was adequate and, for some two years, he opposed the formalising of a learning agreement by committing to writing those things which he and his professors had agreed would be necessary for completion of the degree.

Background

In Chapter 14 I will be discussing a method for implementation of learner managed learning. This method is one which aims at developing participants to the point where they take responsibility for implementing their learning agreement. This is consistent with the move towards psychological maturity that is advocated by Knowles (Chapter 5: '. . . the point at which an individual achieves a concept of essential self-direction is the point of becoming psychologically an adult'). It is consistent also with leadership in general. Manz (1986:585) argues that self-leadership is necessary if people are going to maximise their impact on an organisation and he conceptualises self-leadership as '. . . a comprehensive self-influence perspective that concerns leading oneself towards performance of naturally motivating tasks as well as managing oneself to do work that must be done but is not naturally motivating.'

Within the learning process (particularly if it is goal oriented learning) there is a need to do not only those tasks which one enjoys and finds naturally motivating but also those additional tasks which impact upon ultimate achievement. Thus, for example, a person may want to study psychology or economics but may not enjoy statistical analysis. As long as they can concentrate on the qualitative aspects of either subject they will have no trouble but, if they are to have an adequate understanding of the subject and to develop professional competence, they will need to be able to handle quantitative aspects. Accordingly there is a need for them to gain knowledge and to demonstrate ability in quantitative areas. This requires self-leadership and an essential tool in this process is the learning agreement or learning contract to which reference has been made in several earlier chapters.

It is important at this point to define a learning agreement. A learning agreement or contract is a document in which all parties to the learning process set out the terms and conditions under which the learning is to be done.

Such a document should include the following elements:

1. Introduction, goals, and background information.
2. Proposed activities and methodology.
3. Commitments from each party.
4. Timings.
5. Completion details or closure.

Introduction, goals and background information

Because I see the learning agreement as being a dynamic document to which the learner will refer often during the life of any agreement I encourage the inclusion of these details as a continual reminder to the student of where they have come from and the reason for them undergoing this course of study. If, as I often encounter, the satisfactory completion of one learning agreement is followed by the development of a second, third, or other subsequent agreement, then the inclusion of these sections becomes a valuable history on which the learner can reflect.

Under the introduction I recommend be included a brief statement as to what it is that has brought the learner to this stage in their development. As, in my experience to date, most of those involved in the learner managed learning process are people who either opted out of formal education at an early age or who have returned to study after some years of absence, this section provides an interesting summary of their development in the intervening years.

The next part of this section provides background information as to courses undertaken, formal studies completed, and details of any private reading or study that has impacted upon the present desire for further learning. The intent is to give as rounded a picture as possible of the learner's present level of knowledge and understanding together with information as to the way in which this level has come about.

The final part of this section is to set out the overall goals of the study. The learner needs to set out why they are undertaking this course of study and what they wish to achieve from it. At this stage the goals may not necessarily be a detailed hierarchy in the form shown in Chapter 9 but, at least in overall terms, it will make it very clear as to where the learner is heading.

Proposed activities and methodology

In Chapter 8 I argue that, for learner managed learning, the learner needs to develop the skills which will enable them to determine the instructional techniques that they will find most appropriate. In practical terms, what this means is that the learner needs to determine what courses need to be covered; the sources of such courses; and the agreed methods of assessing satisfactory completion of such courses. Remembering Rogers' contention that, in student-centred learning, 'the requirements for many life situations would be part of the resources the teacher provides' (Rogers 1961:290), it is clear that the facilitative role of the teacher, professor, or trainer is of tremendous value here.

Very often the learner will say that they wish to undergo a course of study but, when one gets to discuss the implications of this desire one discovers that there is little or no real awareness of either the depth of knowledge required or the sources from which such knowledge can be obtained. It becomes essential then that they be guided in these regards especially if they are seeking formal professional qualifications in any field where State or national licensing is required in order to be able to practise. There can be few things more frustrating than a person completing a course of study only to find that they are still not allowed to practise their profession because they have not completed the requirements set out by their professional body or association.

Sometimes the completion of this section will make it clear that, before the desired course of study can be embarked upon, there are certain pre-requisites to be obtained. An example of this may be a person wishing to study medicine or law yet lacking the necessary standardised score results or prior degree. If this occurs the learner is faced with the alternatives of either changing their desired course of study or of extending the envisaged course of study so that the essential pre-requisites are first obtained.

In some respects, this section is almost the 'litmus test' for the goals of the course of study. It tests the true level of motivation from the learner by highlighting specific areas of concern and confronting the learner with the question of whether or not they really wish to proceed with this course of action.

Once the courses to be covered have been determined and all possible sources of such courses are listed, then it becomes possible to lay out a plan showing the timing of such courses in terms of both the order in which courses will be commenced and completed as well as the duration of courses. This enables the learner to ensure that all pre-requisites are met and they do not face the embarrassing situation of, for example, endeavouring to go on to a higher level course in psychology without having completed whatever quantitative analysis, mathematical, or statistical course is a pre-requisite for such a course.

At this stage the learner is not necessarily listing their own timings in detail. They are simply listing the timings required for each course and ensuring that they understand the depth of commitment required if the programme is to be satisfactorily completed.

In my experience the completion of this second stage is the hardest part of developing a learning agreement. Depending on the quality with which this section is completed all other sections will either flow or create problems for the learner. Almost invariably I have found that satisfactory completion of this section requires that the learner goes back and revises the overall goals they have set for the programme to ascertain whether or not they are really achievable goals in light of what is going to be required for them to be met.

Commitments from each party

In Chapter 9 I said that, for learner managed learning to be effective in a corporate context, there needed to be three interactions between the individual, the organisation, and the facilitators. In fact a similar sort of interaction is required in any instance where learner managed learning is to be effective. For organisation one could write academic institution or professional accrediting body and the model would be identical. What I am saying is that there is a high level of commitment required from more than just the learner for learner managed learning to occur. In Chapter 13 I will discuss problems with learner managed learning, and one of these problems relates to the lack of real commitment and support that the learner perceives as being given from their employer, organisation, family and friends, etc.

It is important for the individual to realise that they can only meet part of the commitment required for learning to occur. It is now a truism we recognise that, as John Donne said, 'no man is an island' and this is certainly true in learning. Any programme of learning requires time, money, material resources such as libraries, access to computers, and the like. The learner needs to face the issue of who is going to supply these resources or how they can be obtained. If the learning is to take place within a corporate environment then exactly how much time and money is the employer prepared to commit to the process? If the learner is an employee who is undertaking this learning outside of normal working hours then are there going to be any negative implications for the person's work situation – eg tiredness from long hours spent in study, demands for attendance at a university or college outside of weekends, or the like.

And the learner's family. What are going to be the implications of these demands on the learner's time, money, and emotions in relation to the effect they may have on spouse and/or children? Quite obviously, the longer and more complex the course of study, the more pertinent the questions become and the more essential it becomes that they be faced and dealt with. In instances of people embarking upon very complex courses of study I have found it beneficial to meet with spouses and employers as well as with the learner when assisting in the completion of a learning agreement so as to ensure that all parties have faced up to the ramifications and possible negative effects that are contingent upon such a programme.

Timings

By this stage in development of a learning agreement the learner is quite clear as to the duration and sequence of any courses and they are aware also of the total commitments in time and money that are available to them from the other parties affected by the programme. Armed with this information it now becomes possible for the learner to establish a formal hierarchy of goals and strategies. This is where the requirements of point 2 in Chapter 8 (Goal Setting) are coupled with the hierarchy of goals and strategies set out in Chapter 9. It is the formalising of the appropriate steps that must be taken and the sequence in which they must be taken if the learner is to complete their programme. This action allows for monitoring of the entire process and it will ensure all parties keep their part of the agreement without matters being allowed to drift and any impetus being lost.

Completion details or closure

The purpose of this section is to set out very clearly when the agreement is considered to be at an end. The whole thrust of a learner managed learning programme is on the ultimate achievement of the highest goal in a hierarchy of goals and strategies. With this in mind it is imperative that there be an unambiguous way of ascertaining not only when each level of the hierarchy is met but also when the total programme has reached its conclusion. Especially if the programme is being designed to meet the requirements of a professional body or a formal degree qualification then the closure details will need to be such that the requirements of such bodies are met in an objective and unambiguous manner.

By this means the loop is completed. In the first stage of the agreement we set out the overall goal to be achieved. In the final stage we set out how it is to be ascertained that these goals have been achieved and the programme completed.

Once all these details have been provided then I recommend all parties to the agreement sign it and retain copies of the agreement. Experience indicates that the course of implementing such agreements does not always run smoothly and by ensuring these details are reduced to writing and then signed, later arguments are, if not totally dealt with, then at least somewhat easier to handle as it is clear as to what was agreed upon at the outset.

Not everyone involved in learner managed learning sees the need for agreements as complex as that which I have suggested. Knowles (1984:224) provides a very simple outline for what he terms as 'learning contract' and which I call a 'learning agreement'. Knowles sees the contract as a very valuable means of providing some form of reconciliation between the external needs of an organisation and the internal needs and interests of the learner. He sees it as providing a way of ensuring that, in the move for self-leadership, both the tasks which one finds interesting and the tasks which are not self-motivating are completed. It must be noted though that even in this very simple form of contract Knowles still covers most of the issues that I see as being necessary. His first two steps (diagnosis of learning needs and specifying of objectives) are included in my section of 'introduction, goals, and background information'. His third step (specifying of learning resources and strategies) is dealt with under my 'proposed activities and methodologies' and 'commitments from each party'. His fourth and fifth steps (evidence of accomplishment of objectives and criteria and means for validating evidence) are covered under my headings of 'timings' and 'completion details or closure'. Knowles has certainly as much experience with learning contracts as any other person and, arguably, significantly more experience than any other person in this regard. I believe that he shows how learning agreements can be either very simple or very complex depending on the overall complexity of the programme to be undertaken. Knowles (1984 and 1986) makes it very clear that the document is not a static statement which, once completed is to be filed but rather a dynamic document which becomes an impetus to action and a means of monitoring such action.

I do not believe that there is necessarily a definitive document as regards a learning agreement. I have used a variety of formats – ranging from less than one page through to in excess of a hundred pages in length – depending on the parties involved, the experience of the parties in relation to learner managed learning, the complexity of the study and the requirements of any appropriate professional bodies. Only one thing do I insist upon as being essential: this essential is that the learning agreement be written and signed by all parties.

Martin never did complete his degree through a learner managed learning programme. As time passed the original goals and methodologies became less clear and competing demands for his time coupled with changing interests meant that what he was doing at the end of any year was significantly different from that which he had intended to do at the start of the period. Because he kept no written record of meetings or discussions he questioned the records kept by others with the insistence that his memory was more accurate than notes taken at the time. Eventually we lost contact. I can but hope that he did complete his degree in a more traditional way.

13 Problems with Learner Managed Learning

Case study: *I just can't handle this!*

I first met Kevin in 1982. He had just started on a doctoral programme using learner managed learning. There was no doubt as to Kevin's intellectual ability. He had a bachelor's and master's degree from top universities and currently had his own professional practice. He had his course all mapped out. There was no doubt in his mind (or that of anyone with whom he spoke) that he would progress quickly through the programme and obtain the degree he sought.

In the period to 1985 I had occasion to meet with Kevin some four or five times. There was never any doubt as to his enthusiasm for undertaking the studies nor about his ability to undertake the studies. Despite this it seemed as though he never made any progression. Each time we met I learned of some other problem which had drawn him away from study and which was making it difficult for him to continue. No sooner was one problem solved than another seemed to arise.

I lost contact with Kevin for a few years but, at the end of 1989, I met a mutual friend and, during the course of conversation, the subject of Kevin arose. 'Isn't it a pity,' she said, 'Kevin never did progress with his Degree.'

As has been indicated in previous chapters, there are problems with learner managed learning. It is not the panacea to all ills. I have now been associated with aspects of learner managed learning for some twenty years. Based on my observations over this period it appears to me as though there are six key problem areas:

1. Failure to understand the basic concept;
2. Insufficient task-orientation at the start;
3. The difference between attitude and behaviour;
4. Commitment;
5. Support; and
6. Cultural issues.

Failure to understand the basic concept

I have referred already to the opposition that can be encountered when seeking to introduce learner managed learning. In Chapter 6 I discussed this in relation to perception of threat to the status quo in education and training. Part of this opposition appears to arise because of misunderstanding as to what learner managed learning is all about.

Two common myths related to learner managed learning are:

- that it is something one must do on one's own using whatever technology is required or available; and
- that learner managed learning occurs because a training needs analysis has been conducted and input has been obtained from learners as to their needs and goals.

In relation to the first myth I have explained in several places that learner managed learning can occur in groups; it can involve traditional paradigms; it can use whatever technology is available; but, at the same time, it can have significant amounts of individual learning. Learner managed learning is quite distinct from learning in isolation as well as being distinct from correspondence learning, schools of the air, and the like. It is important to realise this. Very often learning in isolation is really learning under the traditional paradigm, for the student is completing a prescribed course and being examined in a traditional mode as to knowledge rather than competency. In Chapter 11 I looked at the opposition experienced by Carl Rogers when, at Harvard, he promoted the concepts of student centred learning. I contrasted that with the exhilaration Tenenbaum discovered when he implemented the student centred or self-directed approach within the traditional teaching situation. Learner managed learning is student centred learning and, although this may occur in isolation, when properly implemented it challenges the concept of lecturing at students by requiring the facilitator to pay close attention to the needs of each individual student rather than simply to 'students' as a whole.

The second myth is somewhat more insidious and is referred to in both Chapters 3 and 9 because, as discussed in those chapters, a training needs analysis and the involvement of learners in the entire human resource development concept is common in most human resource development functions today. The crucial question as to whether or not such an action is leading to learner managed learning, centres on who is making decisions as to what is learnt and the way in which it is learnt. If the decision-making process and control rests with the teacher or trainer then, almost by definition, the process is going to be centred on that teacher or trainer as the source of information and skill. In learner managed learning the power base moves from the teacher or trainer to the learner. This is discussed in Chapter 6 and it highlights the main difference between schools using the traditional approach and those implementing the new paradigm.

With learner managed learning both the slow learner and the fast learner can be accommodated. This can create additional problems for professional bodies who, working from the traditional base, have come to expect a certain period of time must elapse for suitable learning to be obtained.

An example of this is the Australian Psychological Society who require that a person complete a four year Degree in Psychology together with appropriate supervision for admission as a member of the society. Over that four year period a student will complete other subjects to obtain their degree and, almost certainly, will spend only some 600 hours activity studying psychology. In a learner managed learning mode a person may complete exactly the same quality and quantity of learning in significantly less than four years. In such an instance, under the existing rules of the Australian Psychological Society, such a person may be penalised and stopped from being an accredited professional not because their knowledge and skills are inadequate, but because they have completed the programme in a shorter period than has traditionally been possible. In both instances the core requirements of the learner and the professional body have been ascertained and met but, because of a difference in time-frame, accreditation could be withheld. In this instance, as in the majority of organisational contexts, there would appear to be basic misunderstandings as to the concept of learner managed learning and the way in which it operates.

This problem can be met by changing requirements. Instead of insisting on a four year period of study a professional body such as the Australian Psychological Society could require that applicants for membership pass an examination set by the society and demonstrate their competence through an approved internship. They could conduct these examinations at regular intervals (say three or four times a year) and test knowledge to the level of understanding they would expect from a normal four year degree. If a person could meet those requirements in a period of less than four years then they would not be penalised while the professional standards of the body would not be reduced by allowing membership to inadequately qualified people.

Although I have used the Australian Psychological Society as an example it would be equally possible to use any other professional body. My contention is not that professional standards should be reduced or would be reduced by introducing learner managed learning.

My contention is that, with the increasing use of learner managed learning approaches, it will be necessary for professional bodies to re-define the means by which they assess professional competence in order to allow membership of appropriate bodies. There should be no discrimination between people who complete their qualifications under a traditional paradigm and those who use a learner managed learning approach. Ultimately it is the professional competence of the person that is important as measured by their knowledge, understanding, and ability to implement that which they have studied. If a professional body can be satisfied as to these criteria then it ought not to matter whether they complete their training in two years or twenty years and the problems encountered by professional bodies in regard to applications from people using learner managed learning approaches could be totally alleviated.

Insufficient task-orientation

As I said in Chapter 2, as long as 1931 Alfred North Whitehead was arguing for a change in the approach to the teaching of adults from that which is used to teach children. Around thirty years later Rogers (1961) was providing a model for student-centred teaching and, for at least twenty years, people like Knowles and Nadler have advocated learner managed learning approaches. The work of people such as these has permeated through most of the literature relating to education and training and, for this reason, it is possible to fall into the trap of assuming that learners have some basic understanding of the concepts of learner managed learning and some basic commitment towards it. When these assumptions are made there is a temptation to give less than adequate information as to exactly what learner managed learning is and how it will affect the individual and the organisation.

In the period 1985 through 1987 I taught three times on the Advanced Management Programme conducted by the Australian Institute of Management in New South Wales. In conjuction with this I had the opportunity of observing David Kolb and Ron Fry of Case Western University in their utilisation of learner managed learning as well as teaching alongside Irv Rubin of Situation Management System Inc. The programme we ran was heavily oriented to student-centred learning and encouraging the practice of learner managed learning. The participants on the programme tended to be middle-managers from the public and private sector. Some had formal qualifications others had none. All of them had expectations of attending a programme that would utilise traditional educational and training techniques. At the opening session Ron or David would confront the class with this new approach and, in virtually every case, it was quite apparent that before these people could implement learner managed learning, the 'what', 'how', 'where', and 'who' of learner managed learning needed to be explained. By the time Irv and I moved into our segments it was relatively easy going. The participants had had positive experiences in learner managed learning and they were keen to continue with it.

Where I have worked with individuals and groups who have come into a learning experience knowing that the learner managed learning concept was to be used I have found that there tends to be an enthusiasm for the concept because it sounds different and people think they have an understanding of it but, in reality, there is tremendous ignorance as to the reality of learner managed learning. Invariably new learners expect reasonably large degrees of structure to be provided by the professor and become confused unless a clear understanding of situational leadership is provided.

Hersey and Blanchard (1988) define leadership as being influence and say that whenever we seek to influence a person or a group we are exerting leadership. They go on to talk of leadership in terms of two distinct behaviours. The first of these is task behaviour or the provision of structure which, in their definition, is ensuring that the 'what', 'how', 'when', and 'where' of any task is clearly known. The second aspect is that of relationship behaviour or socio-emotional support. This is the allowing of dialogue, questioning, and the like that ensures the development of understanding and commitment. Their research makes it very clear that, unless appropriate amounts of task behaviour are provided at the outset of any leadership or teaching intervention then any success experienced will be despite the leader rather than because of the leader. (This model will be examined further in Chapter 14 when I look at the implementation of learner managed learning).

It is easy to forget this in learner managed learning. Because one wants to take an andragogical approach then it is possible to fall into the trap of believing it is wrong to spell out specifically what learner managed learning is and how it is to be undertaken. In these instances attempts to implement learner managed learning can fail not because the learners are unwilling to implement learner managed learning but because they do not have a clear understanding of what it is and what it is not. This can lie at the root of failure in learner managed learning programmes.

Attitude versus behaviour

In Chapter 10 the essential interactions for effective human resource development were introduced. I stressed that there must be a commitment in fact rather than simply in theory if learner managed learning is to be implemented. It is this difference between theory and practice that lies at the root of a difference between attitude and behaviour.

Many organisations will agree in principle that human resource development should be implemented and the organisation itself, the human resource development department, and the individuals may also agree, at least in principle, that the principles of andragogy and learner managed learning should be used. The problem comes in seeing this attitude converted into action. If we consider the academic arena then the same is true. The number of people in universities and colleges that I have met who are totally against learner managed learning is few indeed. In fact, over some twenty years, I doubt if they would number more than eight or nine. Accordingly we ought to find a significant movement towards implementation of learner managed learning in most faculties of most universities and colleges. In fact this is not the case. Again the difference is that of converting attitude into action.

It is this conflict between attitude and behaviour that is the primary cause of the perpetuation of a primarily pedagogical approach whether it be in general human resource development or the educational arena. Of course, this conflict between attitude and behaviour is not new nor is it unique to the learning situation. It seems endemic in human nature that far too often there is a discrepancy between that to which we pay lip-service or even really believe to be desirable, and that which we do. For many people the thought of appearing different or doing something that is significantly other than that being done by one's peers or that which is traditionally expected is only possible when the risk of negative consequences for such action is so slight as to be virtually discarded.

If learner managed learning is to be effective then there must be a real commitment that shows itself in action. Those seeking to implement learner managed learning in an organisation or educational institution must ask themselves whether or not they observe behaviour that is consistent with an andragogical approach rather than assuming that a professed attitude will result in the desired behaviour. This observation of behaviour, of course, must be, as Tenenbaum (Chapter 11) acknowledged, an observation of the facilitator's behaviour as well as that of the learner's. If the desired behaviour cannot be observed then steps will need to be taken to ensure that the right behaviour is shown and continues to be shown for learner managed learning to be effective.

What this means is that it is imperative for those wishing to implement learner managed learning that an environment be created in which belief can be put into practice.

Commitment

In the biblical book of Exodus we read that many of the problems of the Israelites (problems which culminated in the Exodus from Egypt) arose because Egypt obtained a new ruler – 'a Pharoah who knew not Joseph'. Similar things happen in relation to learning. In my study on labour turnover (Long 1986) I discuss the psychological aspects of labour turnover and show how frustration in the workplace is a prime factor in this. Often this frustration is caused because a change in top management within an organisation brings about a change in policy so that a programme which has been running very well will falter and fail because it is outside the policy conditions of the new management. I have not done a detailed study of these factors within the educational sectors but, from general observation, it would appear as though exactly the same thing occurs there.

This issue of commitment is a complex one. In many ways this problem is linked with the difference between attitude and behaviour. Dr. Paul Hersey, Chairman of the Leadership Studies Group, often talks about people who 'quit and leave, or, worse still, quit and stay'. The point he makes is that, all to often, people start off with tremendous enthusiasm but then, for a variety of reasons, this enthusiasm wanes and the commitment which once was there is diffused into apathy or antagonism. Any leadership, management, or supervisory behaviour which turns a person from being willing to learn into a person who is unwilling to learn must, to my mind, be at best inappropriate and at worst totally contradictory to the process of developing people. Yet all too often much management and leadership training both in the past and today teaches you how to move a person from being able and willing to being unable and unwilling.

Commitment is double-sided. In Chapter 4 I discussed the environment for learner managed learning and in Chapter 10 I argued that for learner managed learning to be effective in a corporate context there needed to be commitment from the organisation, the individual, and the human resource department/facilitator. It is not enough for the learner to be committed to learner managed learning – if the key people with whom the learner interacts and the environment within which the learner is operating do not share this commitment then the likelihood of the learner remaining committed is significantly lessened. Of course this is not true just of learner managed learning. It is true of most endeavours. Many academically brilliant young people fail to succeed at university because their home environment does not encourage academic pursuits. Similarly many people fail to follow their personal commitments to the arts or the application of a particular skill because their home environment is not conducive to such pursuits. We cannot expect commitment from individuals unless we back up that commitment by support from facilitators, in the home, in the workplace, and in the general educational/learning milieu.

Lack of support

It is possible for there to be commitment in fact as well as in theory by those who interact with the learner, and yet for the support provided to the learner to be inadequate.

Nadler (1982:228) looks at this in relation to general human resource development. He produces a model to illustrate the support that is required before training, during training, and after training. In this model he shows upper management as having involvement in support throughout all of these phases. By this involvement he means that upper management must know what is going on and must demonstrate their support by physically visiting the location in which training is provided and by showing that they are aware of the content of the course. He sees managers and supervisors as being responsible for providing pre-training preparation insofar as they acquaint a trainee as to the reasons why this person is attending a training programme and the results that they expect to achieve through sending the participant on the programme. From here the manager's job is one of job-linkage. During training and after training the manager should be involved in ensuring that participants know how what they have now learned is actually relevant in the work situation. The supervisor has the responsibility, while the participant is away on a training programme, to provide appropriate support including ensuring that the participant's normal workload is not allowed to bank up to the point where training becomes an additional burden. This means that the supervisor has a responsibility to re-allocate workloads so that the work normally carried out by the participant is performed by some other party for the time that the participant is away. After the participant returns from the course then the supervisor has a key responsibility to ensure that the participant is appropriately debriefed so as to ascertain what has actually been learned and how it is to be used in the workplace. The responsibility then is one of ensuring that the participant is able to use this learning in the workplace even if, in the short term, it means that a lower standard of performance is provided during the learning curve of applying training to the real world. Nadler stresses that involvement and support of this nature must be provided if individuals are going to be able to implement their training.

My studies indicate that this is a universal problem. In 1990, as part of my work both with the Centre for Leadership Studies and The Graduate School of Management at Macquarie University, I taught in Finland, Indonesia, Singapore, Hong Kong, Korea, New Zealand, and Australia. In each place this lack of support has been a major problem and barrier to effective learning.

Nadler's experience, like that of most of us involved in human resource development, is that, far too frequently, individuals are told they are to attend a training programme and then, without any prior preparation from their manager, they attend the programme and, at its conclusion, return to work. At that stage little or no reference is made to the programme in terms of its applicability to the work situation and, should there be any loss in productivity as the employee seeks to implement the training, pressure is put upon the participant to maintain previous levels of productivity rather than use the new skills learnt. Nadler argues that real support shows itself by pre-training preparation, support during training, assistance in linking training with the job, and proper follow-up to ensure that training provided is implemented.

Many people regress from enthusiasm and support for learner managed learning to apathy and opposition because of lack of support they have received from those with whom they have had to interact. All persons involved with participants on a learner managed learning programme should be aware of the need for appropriate socio-emotional support and they should spend time with learners seeking to ascertain what support is required and ensuring this is provided.

Cultural issues

In the early 1980s Reginald Smart was one of a group of people who conducted a student-centred-based programme in Singapore.

In a report on this, Smart (1984) raises eighteen issues that created problems within a culture that was significantly different from that in which the programme was delivered. He lists these as:

- An easy style will relax them
- Individual responses to the trainer and the design provide the on-site motivation and compliance necessary in training
- Things are more or less as they seem
- It is both desirable and possible to change 'me'
- Learning is an individual matter, and is optimised when tailored to the individual, and when it springs from his/her own felt needs
- The sky is the limit if you are determined
- Tangible achievements are what matters
- A sensitive trainer will always be aware of conflict
- 'Yes' and 'it's best to tell it like it is'
- Trainers need not to have lived in Asia
- Teasing is a put down
- Average second language competency is enough
- Role playing is a universally useful learning method
- Sensitive Asians will be good 'active listeners'
- Personal disclosure conflicts with the value Asians place on privacy
- The key values to which one can appeal – the currencies of personal influence 'are universal'
- Participants can identify and role play varied responses to their own real-life situations
- A generic behaviour model covers universal influence styles and cultural differences

All these issues, he admits, arose because of a difference in his assumptions about the teaching style to be used for a standard programme in a totally foreign (to him) national culture.

Smart looks at each of these in some depth and he highlights the fact that behaviours and approaches acceptable in one culture do not necessarily make the transition into another culture. His experience was such that he considers the programme he conducted to have been of doubtful real value to the participants although, as a learning experience for himself, it was valuable.

The problems Smart faced are not necessarily going to be faced by every person introducing learner managed learning or aspects thereof in a training programme. However, they do highlight the sorts of issues that need to be considered when one is seeking to introduce learning into any environment. It is quite likely that Smart's Asian participants could have adapted to the learner managed learning concept had more time been taken to familiarise the participants with the concept of learner managed learning and to lead them through it to the point that they could accept it and use it.

The issue of introducing learner managed learning is covered in Chapter 14 but it is interesting to note that, in 1985, some members of a workshop Smart conducted in Australia had difficulty in accepting and implementing the concepts of learner managed learning because it was so vastly different from the traditional pedagogical approach they had experienced in the past. In other words the problems Smart encountered may not necessarily be cross-cultural in relation to oriental versus occidental mind-sets – the problems may relate more to the conflict between learner managed learning and the social learning of any group or individual for which learner managed learning is a new concept.

Copeland (1986:107) in discussing the transfer of knowledge and skills between cultures, says 'the training route is inevitably extremely difficult and rarely satisfying in the short term . . . being taught and civilised by people of another culture does not make it easier.' Copeland argues that the first step is to analyse the 'receiver' country conditions then to become totally aware of the culture and national attitudes prior to commencing any training or education. From here one must then analyse the 'sender' company to ascertain those who have sufficient cross-cultural training to participate in the venture. Even these people will require additional training prior to moving into the new culture and that which is taught will still need to be customised to ensure that cultural differences are minimised. I suggest that this is true for individuals within cultures with which we are familiar as well as with new or different cultures.

Copeland echoes Smart's experience when he says 'the American trainer has a distinct style, which is informal compared to most foreign educator styles, and, unfortunately, many foreigners underestimate or lose respect for the American who violates the local norms.' Just as we must not assume that every individual in our western culture will readily accept and implement learner managed learning neither must we assume that cultural issues can be readily overcome because learner managed learning is seen by us as important. The occidental versus cultural differences must not be played down but at the same time, they must not be used as an excuse for ignoring problems that occur simply because of the totally different paradigm that is expressed by learner managed learning.

If we want learner managed learning to be effective then we will need to take close account of the cultural issues relating to each and every individual so that we can ensure the learning really is student-centred.

Kevin's problems with learner managed learning were varied. He had a reasonable understanding of the basic concept but this could have been increased. He certainly had a very high element of task orientation. However, his main problems related to the difference between attitude and behaviour, the element of commitment from those around, the support he received at home and from his profession, and the cultural issues in relation to his general societal background. It was not Kevin's fault that he dropped out of the programme. He dropped out because he was given no real assistance in confronting and dealing with the very real problems that he encountered.

14 Implementing Learner Managed Learning

Case study: But how?

Laura has just been appointed to the position of associate professor at a major graduate school of management. Part of her responsibility is to introduce a learner managed learning approach for MBA and PhD students.

Laura's academic and professional experience is wide. Between completing her undergraduate studies and her MBA she spent five years working in a highly competitive commercial environment. Following her MBA she spent another four years in a manufacturing environment and then went to Europe for her doctoral studies. This led to three years teaching in the United Kingdom and, prior to her present appointment, she was an assistant professor at a major North American university. It was during her time in North America that Laura first encountered learner managed learning in an academic setting and, once she had made the adjustment to this approach, she found it a very valuable experience. When she applied for her present position one of the things that influenced the selection committee was her exposure to learner managed learning as it was this sort of approach that they wished to implement.

It was just after her appointment that Laura came to me and said, 'Doug, I know what I want to implement. The questions is how do I do it?'

Situational leadership

In Chapter 8 I developed a learner managed learning model and, from there on I have discussed the use of learner managed learning both within and outside of the formal educational context. I have argued that, in the main, there is a widespread knowledge about learner managed learning but somehow that knowledge does not get translated into using the concept. I suggest that a key factor in this non-implementation of learner managed learning is not that people are unwilling to use it, but that they are unsure as to how to implement the concept.

Around 1972 I first encountered Hersey and Blanchard's work on situational leadership. One of the things that impressed me with the model at that time was that it is simple to understand and another was that it has tremendous application as an implementation strategy for the achieving of any goal or result. Particularly over the years since 1980 I have found it a very valuable tool when it comes to implementing learner managed learning.

The basis of situational leadership (Hersey and Blanchard 1988) is that, to be effective, a leader must adapt his or her behaviour to suit the readiness of an individual for a particular task, function, or activity. They define leadership as 'influencing the behaviour of others' and define leadership style as the pattern of behaviour exhibited by a leader as this is perceived by the follower.

In order to maximise leader effectiveness it is necessary to ascertain both the ability and motivation of the follower. In this they reflect totally the model provided by Maier (1973: 329) referred to in Chapter 7. Their argument is that, having ascertained the readiness level of the follower, one then adapts a corresponding leadership style with the assurance that the closer the match between readiness and leadership style the higher the probability of an effective interaction. They stress that the behavioural sciences are a probability science but, from their research over some thirty years, they can produce evidence to support the validity of their model. The situational leadership model is reproduced at Figure 7.

In using this model under any circumstances there are three things to determine:

1. What is the precise task, function, activity, goal, or result that is to be done or is sought?
2. In relation to this specific task etc what is the demonstrated level of ability – ie knowledge, experience, skill – that is exhibited?
3. In relation to this task etc what is the level of willingness, confidence, motivation that is exhibited for performing the task?

Using the model it becomes clear that, if the person's readiness for learner managed learning is low, then the style with the highest probability of success is a high task/low relationship intervention. This means that, for such a person, there will need to be a lot of instruction as to the what, how, where, when, and who of the learner managed learning process.

In Chapter 13 when I spoke of one of the problems relating to learner managed learning as being inadequate task orientation at the start of the process, this is the specific intervention to which I refer. A person may have a very high degree of commitment to learner managed learning in terms of their motivation to learn but, until they know what

Figure 7 *The situational leadership model*

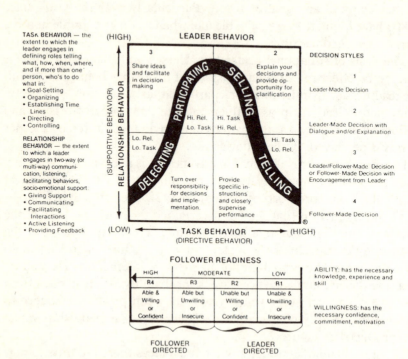

TASK BEHAVIOR — the extent to which the leader engages in defining roles telling what, how, when, where, and if more than one person, who's to do what in:
• Goal-Setting
• Organizing
• Establishing Time Lines
• Directing
• Controlling

RELATIONSHIP BEHAVIOR — the extent to which a leader engages in two-way (or multi-way) communication, listening, facilitating behaviors, socio-emotional support:
• Giving Support
• Communicating
• Facilitating Interactions
• Active Listening
• Providing Feedback

When a Leader Behavior is used appropriately with its corresponding level of readiness, it is termed a *High Probability Match*. The following descriptors can be useful when using Situational Leadership for specific applications:

S1	S2	S3	S4
Telling	Selling	Participating	Delegating
Guiding	Explaining	Encouraging	Observing
Directing	Clarifying	Collaborating	Monitoring
Establishing	Persuading	Committing	Fulfilling

Source: From Paul Hersey, Kenneth H. Blancard, *Management of Organizational Behavior: Utilizing Human Resources*, Fifth Edition 1988, Prentice Hall, Inc., Englewood Cliffs, New Jersey 07632, Page 182. Used with permission.

learner managed learning is all about, their attempts to implement the process are likely to involve considerable amounts of trial and error. Accordingly there is a reasonable degree of insecurity caused by this lack of concrete knowledge. Under such circumstances a person may succeed in implementing the process – and countless examples can be listed where this is the case – but, to my mind, the downside of this risk – ie the likelihood that the person will be turned off from the concept of learner managed learning and lifelong development – is so great as to render it unacceptable. Accordingly, by using this high task/low relationship intervention we are able to ensure that the learner understands the basic concept, receives appropriate task orientation at the start, and is alerted to the fact that implementing learner managed learning is essential – ie they learn the distinction between attitude and behaviour in this instance.

Using this model, as the learner exhibits growth in understanding and implementing the learner managed learning process then, by means of positive reinforcement, it becomes possible to help the person grow from a low level of readiness through to the first of the moderate levels of readiness. It is at this stage that the learner will benefit from a high task and high relationship intervention. The learner will require much assistance in matters such as the developing of a learning agreement (see Chapter 12) and, almost certainly, will need encouragement as the realisation strikes that learner managed learning is probably the hardest form of education with which to involve oneself. It is at this point that the issues of commitment, support, and cultural issues will need to receive most attention. This is the stage at which the learner knows enough about the basic concepts of learner managed learning to be able to ask questions relating to the way it is implemented. Accordingly the facilitator will need both to provide specific information in answer to questions as well as to encourage the learner in the development of a learning agreement and the actual implementation of the learner managed learning process.

Once the learning agreement is completed then the learner is able to continue on the learner managed learning process but now requires encouragement and support as they move further away from the traditional paradigm. Accordingly at the upper level of moderate levels of readiness it is not necessary to provide large amounts of task behaviour but the learner requires support in terms of sharing information and an awareness that other people understand the issues relating to learner managed learning and are willing to provide assistance when and where this is required.

Providing this supportive stage occurs, my experience is that, almost without fail, the learner is able to make the transition through to the point of being able to stand on their own and the learner managed learning process operates effectively with a true commitment to the concept of lifelong learning being obtained. Accordingly, as the learner moves through to the highest level of readiness – that of being able, willing, and confident, the facilitator's role moves to one of minimal amounts of task and relationship behaviour – ie provision of support only as this is specifically requested by the learner. However, one must note that, at this point, the review aspects that were set out in the learning agreement are important as it is the way in which these are implemented that will provide the necessary reviews for the learner to grow and develop in their total commitment to lifelong learning.

In Chapter 8 I introduced a model of learner managed learning which showed the movement from a basically behavioural approach through to a cognitive approach to learning as the overall readiness of the learner develops. This model is reproduced at Figure 8 and it can be seen readily that there is a congruity between the two models.

When these two models are compared it can be seen that, while the learner is on the lower levels of readiness the positive reinforcement from an external party or parties has greatest likelihood of helping them through the learning process. As they move through the higher levels of readiness then the reinforcement comes from within and the cognitive aspects of learning become more operative and effective.

Situational leadership in practice

Although the situational leadership model is primarily a model which applies to individuals, it also has application at a group situation. Accordingly, it is possible to use this model for implementation of learner managed learning whether one be working with an individual or group. Consider the following example.

In July 1985 I was approached by the Australian subsidiary of an American multinational to introduce a training programme. I was given the following information:

In 1980 the organisation employed 15 people in Australia and had 500 units of business. As at July 1985 they employed 27 people and had 3,500 units of business. By 1990 it was their intention to employ approximately 40 people and have 7,000 units of business. The annual turnover of the organisation was in the multimillions and, in a highly competitive market, it was the most profitable of its kind within Australia. The organisation had identified 11 people they saw as being the key to the future of the organisation in Australia. None of these had academic qualifications and, in fact, most had left school without completing their secondary education. Most were currently employed in either a sales or clerical function. The

TEACHING STRATEGIES

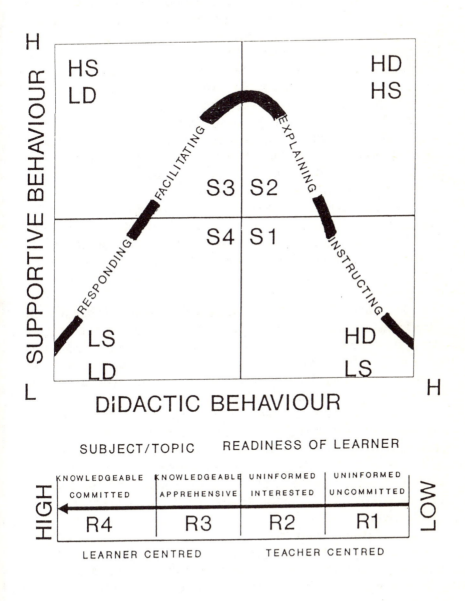

Figure 8 *The learner managed learning model*

organisation wished to have these 11 people brought to the point where they could qualify for entry to a degree programme within five years

In this event the client organisation knew exactly where they were as at July 1985 and they had clearly identified and enunciated their goals to the year 1990. Accordingly, the first two steps towards introducing learner managed learning had been taken and completed by the client. The next stage was to identify the current level of knowledge and understanding for each participant (ie at this stage, in terms of situational leadership, the current level of job relevant maturity or readiness for each participant was being ascertained). This was done by preparing a questionnaire that the general manager personally took to each of the eleven and, when giving it to the person, explained what was being done and the rationale behind it. Each questionnaire had the name and address of the respondent and they were returned directly to the co-ordinator. In light of the fact that the chief executive officer himself took these questionnaires around and explained what was taking place it is not surprising that there was a 100 per cent return. Each respondent felt that the organisation was totally committed to the prospect of learner managed learning. These replies were collated and a basic working paper explaining the philosophy of the programme was then prepared and distributed to each respondent.

At this juncture two text books were selected and provided to each participant as a means of providing a common language and base for the group. Their attention was drawn to specific chapters and it was explained to them how the programme was intended to work. (In terms of situational leadership, the approach was high task – low relationship so they could know what, how, when, where, and who as this applied to learner managed learning.) This was followed by personal contact with each of the eleven in order to deal with issues and concerns that arose. It was stressed to each participant that their own programme would be driven by themselves. Their attitude to the concept of learner managed learning was ascertained and it was pointed out that no commitment to this programme would be made until after each individual had had the chance to provide input and deal with appropriate issues at a forthcoming workshop. (In terms of situational leadership, as the participants demonstrated increasing ability in terms of satisfactorily performing initial tasks of reading appropriate chapters and completing a questionnaire, they were given reinforcement by means of personal attention and a one-to-one explanation of what was involved and how we would be proceeding.) At the workshop held in November 1985, we spent a week in which the various questions and issues raised by each person could be dealt with both on a one-to-one and on a group basis and, over the course of the week, participants developed their learning agreements. The actual process used to do this started by getting each participant to re-write their job descriptions in results-oriented terms. This created some difficulty as there was a temptation for them to think and write in terms of activities rather than in the measures by which they were to be assessed. In fact, this proved the hardest part of the entire programme and took significantly longer than had originally been envisaged. Once these job descriptions had been re-written and agreed upon between each participant and the chief executive, specific learning goals and objectives were set with each person. When these were agreed subordinate goals, each clearly defined in results-oriented terms, were set and a curriculum was devised for each participant. A monitoring system was set up in which each participant would report back on a regular basis to the chief executive as to the results achieved and the current stage of each step. All of this was then set out in the learning agreement.

Initially there was a temptation to try and do too much too quickly. This was dealt with by ensuring each person had a realistic idea of the time available and their own capabilities. In order to reach this it was essential that a high relationship/high task intervention be provided on both a one-on-one and group basis.

Throughout the conference the role of the consultant was that of a resource and facilitator. It was necessary initially to provide large amounts of structure as and when this was appropriate but, as the readiness level of individuals and the group developed, decreasing amounts of structure and increasing amounts of relationship behaviour were provided. In fact, the times at which the consultant provided more task behaviour than was appropriate because he failed to recognise the growing maturity of an individual or the group, were the times when the process ran the greatest danger of being thwarted. In this way it was a learning experience for both participants and the facilitator.

The curricula devised took into account both the organisational and individual goals. As each of the participants was responsible for achieving budgeted results, the programme concentrated on developing skills that would assist in the attaining of these results. It must be stressed that, throughout the process, the driving force moved away from the consultant and the chief executive over to the participants. Eventually all changes and input was in direct response to their requests for assistance.

Over the past five years there have been many changes in that organisation. Many of the eleven have left the organisation because of general turmoil that has occurred both within that particular industry and the industries to which it is closely aligned. Despite that it is encouraging to note that seven of the eleven maintain personal contact with me and, as at the start of 1990, are continuing on a learner managed learning programme that is basically the same as that on which they embarked in 1985. Two of these are now embarked on formal academic studies.

In Chapter 11 I quoted Rogers (1961) who, on the subject of student-centred learning, says '. . . the requirements for many life situations would be part of the resources the teacher provides. The teacher would have available the knowledge (of) . . . requirements set, not by the teacher, but by life. The teacher is there to provide the resources which the student can use to learn so as to be able to meet these tests.' This is certainly the case with the people in the example given. When each of these left school they had the belief that they could progress through their working life with the minimal education obtained from three or less years of secondary schooling. It was as they moved from basically clerical or selling occupations into management that they realised the need not only for an experiential awareness of issues such as financial management, marketing, human resource management, planning, and the like but also for a formal understanding of the foundations on which experience was based so that, given the vagaries of real life, they would have adequate knowledge and understanding to be able to apply these foundations in ways most conducive to the efficacious conducting of business. Their impetus for learning came not from the chief executive officer but from themselves. It was in response to their requests for ongoing training that he sought a means by which they could receive the education they required. Accordingly, although at school they had been indifferent learners, when a little older (their ages ranged from 23 to 35) they readily embraced the opportunity for study and, for the most part, have been successful in their quest for formal knowledge.

This example, of course, is used for learner managed learning within an organisational setting. The same process, however, is equally applicable outside of an organisational setting. Central to any implementation of learner managed learning is the need first to assess the current level of knowledge and willingness of the learner and then to adapt one's style of influence to that which most closely matches this observed readiness level. In this way it becomes possible (as was discussed in Chapter 7) to channel an individual's motivation to learn into an experience which becomes positive in that quest for personal development which is essential for lifelong learning and development – that which Rogers sees as central to 'becoming a person'.

It was this model that Laura decided to use at the university. In her first class she explained to her students the process she intended to use and the general principles of learner managed learning. She then asked each student to write an essay in which they gave their current level of understanding relating to the subject and this was followed by one-on-one discussions with each student that, eventually, culminated in a learning agreement being signed. As at the time of writing it is too early to say how the overall implementation of this process will go but, at least to date, there is a reasonable level of enthusiasm and commitment from her students.

15 Where To From Here?

Case study: *Can I?*

Oliver is now 49 years old. It is more than 25 years since he completed his last formal education but, since then, he has had a successful managerial career in three countries. Eighteen months ago he joined his present organisation as deputy chief executive and, since then, he has been encouraged to resume formal education. He knows something of the principles of learner managed learning but he was concerned about all that could be involved and the way in which it would affect him.

The challenge of learner managed learning

Handy (1985:238) says:

Many organisations do not change; they only fade away and others grow up to take their place. Unable to contemplate a future different from all that they have been used to, they continue to beaver away at what they know best how to do, working harder and more efficiently at a diminished task. Education, for instance, is the growth sector of every society, yet in Britain schools are contracting or closing and the educational profession is in recession and retreat; meanwhile, computer manufacturers, book publishers, video film makers, language schools, and above all, the Manpower Services Commission of the Department of Employment, are booming away. Education, yes, but not in schools, it seems. Indeed, as educational networks become more common and more available we may see the school leaving age reduced, leaving individuals, perhaps financed by vouchers, to choose their own sources of learning while schools contract even more . . .

Unusually, however, and fortunately, their destiny is in their own hands.

Handy seems to summarise much of the emphasis I have sought to make in this book. Our society today is questioning seriously the traditional paradigm of education and training. Questions are being asked as to the relevance of education. More than ever before executives are experiencing mid-career crises. People making contributions in all walks of life are dropping out of traditional educational processes because they see them as restrictive rather than developmental. Many of our graduates from all levels of formal education are obtaining large amounts of knowledge – much of which they are neither equipped or able to use outside of narrow academic areas. Organisations such as the Club of Rome and The Centre of Continuing Education in Canberra are examining the status quo and finding need for change. We know where we are. We have a picture of traditional education and training as it exists in the late twentieth century. The question we have to face is 'where to from here?'

Richard Bolles (1978) suggests that there are three boxes of life. These are:

1. The world of education.
2. The world of work.
3. The world of retirement.

He looks at the imbalance that exists between these three plus the fact that we tend to see them as three independent variables. Bolles' solution as to how we get out of these three boxes of life is to get involved in lifelong learning. The first decision that has to be made, however, is whether or not we want to get out of these boxes. This question is closely related to that of where we go from here. It is necessary for all of us involved in the field of human development to make a decision as to whether or not we want to change the status quo and, if we do want to change it, what are the goals that we are going to set. If we are going to change the status quo, what are we going to change it to?

Thus we are brought again to the very basis of learner managed learning. Decisions of this nature are not the sort that can be superimposed from outside. A modernist philosophy of human nature is inappropriate here. If change is going to come then it must be in accord with the hermeneutic view of human nature which sees the changes being directed and being controlled from within the individual so that all assessment and reinforcement is internally driven. Unless each of us individually wants to bring about some aspect of change in the educational paradigm in which we operate then it is unlikely that long-term effective change will occur. If we are to become involved in learner managed learning and lifelong learning then there needs to be an individual commitment to it rather than assent to a theoretical construct.

Learner managed learning is not a fad. In their statement of intent, The Centre for Continuing Education (1984) list eight criticisms of recurrent education. Because they come from a position within the traditional education environment, most of those listed are not totally relevant to the concept of lifelong learning. However, the criticism they list as the most substantial of these is 'recurrent education is a radical strategy for the transformation of the education system. Radical change naturally disturbs existing interests. It may be expected to encounter overt and covert resistance, whether from those who prefer their students and employees docile and dependent or from those who simply prefer not to have to make the effort to do things differently.'

This criticism is even more vehement for learner managed learning. The Centre for Continuing Education does not advocate the development of a parallel, rival, or compensatory system, alongside the existing structure but, as already stated in Chapter 2, an argument can be made for the introduction of such a system. Lifelong learning as proposed here supports the possible introduction of such an alternative system although, as argued, it does not make such an alternative system mandatory.

Experience within both the United States of America and Australia indicates that there is a need for an educational system based on the principle of learning being a lifelong experience in which individuals take an increasing responsibility for their own development. It is an activity that shows very high concern for task (developing individuals so that goals can be met) while at the same time showing an extremely high concern for people (socio-emotional support that seeks to start at the current level of knowledge and understanding exhibited by the learner) and it uses experiential learning as a key means of imparting knowledge.

The concept is not new and, in fact, aspects of it have been used extensively for many years. Trainers have advocated experiential learning since at least the early 1970s and most trainers and educators would agree that it is an extremely valuable means of imparting knowledge. However, the full implementation of learner managed learning does not yet appear to be widely accepted. Our secondary and tertiary education sectors seem to have a predisposition to the pedagogical approach and, as most trainers and educators are themselves products of this system, it is not surprising that pedagogy is still to be found more frequently than andragogy in training situations.

In considering recurrent education, The Centre for Continuing Education states '. . . we can but assert that recurrent education is important since educational reconstruction is indicated on several fronts for creating an attractive future.' This is especially true if the concept of lifelong learning is to be introduced. The paper goes on to examine the programme focus and says:

It will have to analyse the trends and forces in the political, economic, administrative and social spheres which appear to favour and to obstruct the envisaged changes. This would include asking questions about and analysing the following kinds of issues:

1. The present policies and commitments of political parties, of the governments of the day, and of the relevant sectors of the Commonwealth and State bureaucracies.
2. Attitudes and preferences of the general community, especially but not only as parents, often reflected or distorted by the media.
3. The current operation of the Australian Federal system with its division of powers between Federal and State levels, which makes the co-ordination and implementation of policy harder than in the unitary system.
4. Economic circumstances, and assumptions about these, especially of education as conceived as a consumption item, and indulgence compared with capital investment; or of recurrent education as seen as implying investment in sectors of the community which promise a poorer return than investment elsewhere.
5. Culture, tradition, and established practice, for instance, the custom of importing skilled labour which may militate against the idea of periodic retraining, or re-investment in human resources to maintain and update skills.

They go on to list the various groups which may resist changes in the direction of recurrent education because of perceived threats to traditional advantages. They list the vested interests of professional associations and trade unions, the education system, employer organisations and associations, and the formation of alliances between these groups. As has been illustrated in previous chapters, the possibility of this opposition is very real.

There is no doubt that continuing with the traditional approach is significantly easier than the introduction of learner managed learning. The traditional approach enhances the power base of the teacher who is seen as the source of knowledge with a power aimed at influencing opinion and attitude. Bertrand Russell (1938) said 'the most important organisations are approximately distinguishable by the kind of power they exert. The army and the police exercise cohesive power over the body; economic organisations, in the main, use rewards and punishments as incentives and deterrents; schools, churches, and political parties aim at influencing opinion. But these distinctions are not very clear-cut, since every organisation uses other forms of power in addition to the one which is most characteristic.'

Learner managed learning challenges this concept of power. It moves the power base away from the teacher or trainer and gives it to the learner. In so doing it challenges the premise that we, as 'authorities', know what is best for our people and what is necessary for our organisation.

In light of such a challenge the opposition to learner managed learning is not surprising. In a society which seeks shorter working hours for increased remuneration and in which competitiveness and education, sport, and commerce is either implicitly or explicitly discouraged by politicians and pressure groups, it is easier to maintain the status quo no matter what benefits may accrue from a change.

Learner managed learning is an exciting concept and, where it is implemented correctly, it brings benefits to individuals and organisations.

The need for a new mind-set

Hilmer (1985) talks about requiring a 'new mind-set'. He explains a mind-set as being the way in which a person feels, interprets, communicates, and acts. Our mind-sets are assumptions about the people and the world around us. They help us decide whether the smile we see on a person's face is a greeting or a mockery. Our mind-set may or may not give us the inspiration to summon the extra effort to win a tennis match. It is our mind-set or attitude that will act as a filter or amplifier and give meaning to the barrage of words and signals we receive every day.

Where do mind-sets come from? They begin to form in us as children and are developed and reinforced by what we observe, are told, and experience.

He goes on to suggest that Australia had a 'conscript' mind-set in which people were not asked or expected to make any kind of thoughtful contribution to their work but simply forced to do it. He contrasts this with the United States of America which also began as a penal colony and yet in which a totally different approach to work and life has developed. Hilmer contrasts the conscript way of thinking with the 'volunteer' mind-set which is based on the premise that given the right conditions people can and will make positive contributions to their work. He sees these as people who enjoy what they do and who make the choice to take initiatives and to do a good job. Hilmer goes on to argue that, if Australia is to grow or even maintain its current stature internationally there is a need to change the mind-set from the conscript to the volunteer.

A similar argument can be made in terms of learning within Australia. As long as we continue with a traditional approach that encourages a mind-set in which we are dependent upon third parties for determining our learning goals, our learning experiences, and our learning methodologies we will continue to develop a society in which protectionism is paramount. A change to the self-directed mind-set will ensure that we develop people who have a concept of essential self-direction which, in Knowles terms, is the mark of being psychologically an adult.

Of course, much of what I say is applicable not only to Australia. I have focused on Australia because this is the country in which I live but, as shown from the examples listed above and as argued in many of the sources cited, the issues that must be confronted are not unique to Australia – they are universal issues. The tragedy is that, all too often, we have buried our heads in the sand and hoped they would go away rather than confronting them and bringing about the change that is so urgently desired.

In part it may be that the reason for this failure to implement learner managed learning is because the Olivers of this world are numerous. There is some vague understanding of learner managed learning and the way at which it can be implemented but, far too often, the in depth understanding and impetus to action is lacking. Oliver is now embarking on a doctoral programme using the principles of learner managed learning. In part his question to me prompted this book. Hopefully the material provided to him will be of benefit to others.

Bibliography

Agor, W L (1986) 'The Logic of Intuition: How Top Executives Make Important Decisions', *Organizational Dynamics*, Periodicals Division, American Management Association, Winter 1986

Bandura, A (1977) *Social Learning Theory*, New Jersey, Prentice-Hall

Bandura, A and Walter, R H (1959) *Adolescent Aggression*, New York, Ronald

Bennis, W (1985) *The Planning of Change*, New York, Harper & Row

Blanchard, K and Lorber, R (1984) *Putting the One Minute Manager to Work*, New York, William Morrow & Company

Bock, D (1986), quoted in West, W, 'Harvard Head's Lament over Ways of Learning', *The Australian*, September 17, 1986

Bolles, R N (1978) *The Three Boxes of Life and How to Get Out of Them*, Berkeley, California, Ten Speed Press

Botkin, J W, Elmadjra, M and Malitza, M (1979) *No Limits to Learning Bridging the Human Gap – a Report to the Club of Rome*, Oxford, Pergamon Press

Boyer, E L (1987) *College. The Undergraduate Experience in America*, New York, Harper & Row

Byrd, J and Moore, LT (1982) *Decision Models for Management*, New York, McGraw Hill Inc

Centre for Continuing Education (1984) *Recurrent Education for Australia: Statement of Intent*, Recurrent Education Programme, The Australian National University, May 1984

Clavell, J (1963) *The Children's Story . . . But Not Just for Children*, New York, Dell Publishing Co

Copeland, L (1986) 'Skills Transfer and Training Overseas', *Personnel Administrator*, Vol 31, No 6, June 1986

Dalton, GW & Thompson, PH (1986) *Novations: Strategies for Career Management*, Glenview, Illinois, Scott, Foresman and Company

Dewsbury, DA (1984) *Comparative Psychology in the Twentieth Century*, Pennsylvania, Hutchinson Ross Publishing Company

Eisenhardt, KM (1990) 'Speed and Strategic Choice: How Managers Accelerate Decision Making', Berkeley, CA, *California Management Review*, Vol 32, No 3

Etzioni, A (1961) *A Comparative Analysis of Complex Organisations*, New York, Free Press

Eysenck, HJ (1965) *Fact and Fiction in Psychology*, Harmondsworth, Penguin Books

French, RP, Raven, B and Cartwright, D (1959) 'The Bases of Social Power' in Cartwright, D (ed) *Studies in Social Power*, University of Michigan, Ann Arbor, pp 150–67

Handy, C (1985) *Gods of Management*, London, Pan Books

Hersey, P and Blanchard, K (1988) *Management of Organizational Behaviour: Utilizing Human Resources*, 5th edition, New Jersey, Prentice-Hall

Hilmer, FG (1985) *When the Luck Runs Out*, Sydney, Harper & Row

Hunt, JW (1979) *Managing People at Work*, London, McGraw Hill

(1981) *Managers in Mid-Career: Summary of Results*, Regents Park, London Business School

(1981) *Mid Career Crises*, Regents Park, London Business School

Jackson, MW and Prosser, MT (1986) 'Why Lecturing and Exams don't Teach', *Sydney Morning Herald*, September 17, 1986

Jaques, E (1965) Death and the Mid-Life Crisis, *International Journal of Psychoanalysis*, Vol 46

Jung, C (1933) *Modern Man in Search of a Soul*, New York, Harcourt Brace

Kabuga, C (1977) 'Why Andragogy?' Adult Education and Development, September, 1977. Reproduced as 'Andragogy in Developing Countries' in Knowles, M (1984) *The Adult Learner: A Neglected Species*, 3rd edition, Houston, Texas, Gulf Publishing Company

Kets de Vries, M (1978) 'The Mid-Career Conundrum', *Organisational Dynamics*, autumn 1978

Knowles, MS (1970) *The Modern Practice of Adult Education – Andragogy versus Pedagogy*, New York, Association Press

(1975) *Self Directed Learning: A Guide for Learners and Teachers*, New York, Cambridge Books

(1984) *The Adult Learner: A Neglected Species*, 3rd edition, Texas, Gulf Publishing Company

(1986) *Using Learning Contracts*, San Francisco, Jossey Bass

Koestler, A (1975) *The Ghost in the Machine*, London, Pan Books

Kolb, DA and Boyatzis, RE (1984) 'Goal Setting and Self Directed Behaviour Change, in Kolb, DA, Rubin, IM and McIntyre,

JM *Organisational Psychology: Reading on Human Behaviour in Organisations*, 4th edition, New Jersey, Prentice-Hall

Kolb, DA. and Fry, R (1975) 'Toward an Applied Theory of Experiential Learning' in *Theories of Group Processes*, Cooper, GL (ed), New York, John Wiley & Sons

Kolb, DA, Rubin, IM and McIntyre, JM (1984) *Organizational Psychology: An Experiential Approach to Organizational Behaviour*, New Jersey, Prentice-Hall

Kouzes, JM. and Posner, BE (1987) *The Leadership Challenge: How to Get Extraordinary Things Done in Organizations*, San Francisco, Jossey Bass

Kramer, L (1986) 'The Tyranny of Relevance', *The Australian Director, Journal of the Institute of Directors in Australia*, Vol 16, No 3, June/July 1986

Leach, DJ and Raybould, EC (1977) *Learning and Behaviour Difficulties in School*, London, Open Books

Levinson, D (1978) *Seasons of a Man's Life*, New York, Alfred Knopf

Levinson, D et al (1976) 'Periods in the Adult Development of Men', *The Counselling Psychologist*, Vol 6, No 1

Levinson, H (1969) 'On Being a Middle Aged Manager', *Harvard Business Review*, July/August 1969

Likert, R (1961) *New Patterns of Management*, New York, McGraw Hill

Livingstone, JS (1969) 'Pygmalion in Management', *Harvard Business Review*, July/August 1969, pp 81–2

Locke, EA (1968) 'Towards a Theory of Task Motivation and Incentives', *Organisational Behaviour and Human Performance*, Vol 3, pp 157–89

(1975) 'Personnel Attitudes and Motivation', *Annual Review of Psychology*, Vol 26

(1977) 'The Myths of Behaviour Mod in Organisations', *Academy of Management Review*, October 1977.

(1978) 'The Ubiquity of the Technique of Goal Setting in Theories of and Approaches to Employee Motivation', *Academy of Management Review*, July 1978.

Long, DG 1982 'The Effect of Labour Turnover on the HRD. Function', *Training and Development in Australia, The Australian Institute of Training and Development*, Vol 9, No 3, September 1982.

(1982) 'Towards More Effective use of Human Resources', *Professional Administrator, the Australian Division, The Institute of Chartered Secretaries and Administrators*, Vol xxxiv, No 5, December 1982

(1985) 'Improving Results Through People', *The Australian Director, Journal of the Institute of Directors in Australia*, Vol 15, No 6, December 1985/January 1986

(1986) 'A Leap Forward in Self-directed Training', *An interview, AIM, Australian Institute of Management NSW Limited*, No 1, February 1986

(1986) *Labour Turnover in the Australian Economy: Indications of Its Causes, Costs and Possible Control*, Ann Arbor, Michigan, University Microfilms International

(1989) 'Leadership in Corporate Management', Sydney, Centre for Leadership Studies

Lusterman, S (1977) Education Industry, *The Conference Board Report*, No 719, New York, The Conference Board Inc

Maier, NRF (1973) *Psychology in Industrial Organisations*, 4th edition, Boston, Houghton Mifflin

Manz, CC (1986) 'Self Leadership: Towards an Expanded Theory of Self-Influence Processes in Organisations' *Academy of Management Review*, Vol 11, No 3

Maslow, A (1968) *Toward a Psychology of Being*, 2nd edition, New York, Van Nostraad Reinhold

McClelland, DC (1966) 'That Urge to Achieve', originally published in *Think* published by IBM Corporation 1966, 82–9, reproduced in *Classic of Organizational Behaviour* (1978) Walter E Natemeyer (ed), Oak Park, I11, Moore Publishing,

(1970) 'The Two Faces of Power', *Journal of International Affairs*, Vol 24, No 1

McGregor, D (1960) *The Human Side of Enterprise*, McGraw-Hill Book Company

Merrill, DW and Reid, H (1981) *Personal Styles & Effective Performance*, Radnor, PA, Chilton Book Company

Molander, C (1976) 'The Mid-life Crisis', *Cranfield Management Review*, Vol 1, No 1

Moloney, C (1982) *Training as it exists in France*, unpublished paper presented to conference of trainers, Sydney, Australia, April 20, 1982

Nadler, L (1980) *Corporate Human Resources Development: A Management Tool*, Van Nostrand, Reinhold Company

(1982) *Designing Training Programs The Critical Events Model*, Philippines, Addison-Wesley

Nadler, L and Wiggs GD (1986) *Managing Human Resource Development*, San Francisco, Jossey Bass

Newstrom, JW and Scannell, EE (1980) *Games Trainers Play: Experiential Learning Exercises*, McGraw Hill

(1983) *More Games Trainers Play*, McGraw Hill

OECD (1973) *Recurrent Education: A Strategy for Lifelong Learning*, Paris, OECD.

Pascal, AH (1975) *An Evaluation of Policy Related Research on Programmes for Mid-Life Career Redirection*, Vol 1 – Executive Summary, Rand, Santa Monica

Pavlov, IP (1927) *'Conditioned Reflexes'* GV Anrep, Trans, Oxford, Oxford University Press

Peccei, A 1979 'No Limits to Learning', in Botkin, JW, Elmandjra, M & Malitza, M *No Limits to Learning – Bridging the Human Gap – a Report to the Club of Rome*, Oxford, Pergamon Press

Peters, T (1987) *Thriving on Chaos*, London, Pan Books

Pfeiffer, JW and Jones, JE (1968) *A Handbook of Structured Experiences for Human Relations Training*, La Jolla, California, University Associates

Rackham, N and Morgan, T (1977) *Behaviour Analysis in Training*, UK, McGraw-Hill

Robinson, RB and Pearce, JA (1988) Planned Patterns of Strategic Behaviour and Their Relationship to Business-Unit Performance, *Strategic Management Journal*, Vol 9, No 1

Rogers, CR (1961) *On Becoming a Person*, Boston, Houghton Mifflin

(1970) *Encounter Groups*, Harmondsworth, Penguin Books

Rogers, MF (1973) 'Instrumental and Infra-Resources: The Bases of Power', *American Journal of Sociology*, Vol 79, No 6

Roskin, R (1984) 'Choosing Experiential Based Learning Designs for Management Development', *The Journal of Management Development*, Vol 3, No 2., MCB, Bradford, University Press

Ross, I (1986) 'Corporations Take Aim at Illiteracy', Vol 114, No 7, *Fortune International*, September 29, 1986

Russell, B (1938) *Power: A New Social Analysis*, London, Unwin

Skinner, BF (1938) *The Behaviour of Organisms*, New York, Appleton-Century-Crofts

(1971) *Beyond Freedom and Dignity*, New York, Knopf

(1974) *About Behaviourism*, New York, Knopf

Smart, R (1984) *Using an American Learning Model in Asia: A Case Study*, unpublished report, Long Beach, California, California State University

Sofer, C (1970) *Men in Mid-Career: A Study of British Managers and Technical Specialists*, Cambridge, CUP

Stata, R (1989) 'Organizational Learning – The Key To Management Innovation', *Sloan Management Review*, Vol 30, No 3

Stones, D (1966) *An Introduction to Educational Psychology*, London, Methuen

Sullivan, J (1986) 'Human Nature, Organization, and Management Theory', *The Academy of Management Review*, Vol 11, No 3, July 1986

Tenenbaum, S (1961) As quoted by Rogers, C (1961) *On Becoming a Person*, Boston, Houghton Mifflin, p 311

Thorndike, EL (1905) *The Elements of Psychology*, New York, Seiler

Toffler, A (1970) *Future Shock*, London, Pan Books

(1981) *The Third Wave*, London, Pan Books

(1986) 'Beyond the Breakup of Industrial Society: Political and Economic Strategies in the Context of Upheaval', in *The Leader-Manager*, JN Williamson (ed), 1986, New York, John Wiley & Sons

Tolman, EG (1949) *Purposive Behaviour in Animals and Men*, Berkeley, University of California Press

Vroom, VH (1964) *Work and Motivation*, New York, John Wiley & Sons

Wolfe, DM and Kolb, DA (1984) 'Career Development, Personal Growth, and Experiential Learning' in Kolb, Rubin and McIntyre, *Organisational Psychology: Readings on Human Behaviour in Organisations*, 4th edition, New Jersey, Prentice-Hall

Worell & Nelson (1974) *Managing Instructional Problems: A Case Study Work Book*, McGraw-Hill

Yuill, B (1980) *From Theory to Practice in the Assessment of Organisations*, Monograph Published by Royal Melbourne Institute of Technology, May 6, 1980.

Yukl, GA (1989) *Leadership in Organisations*, 2nd edition, New Jersey, Prentice-Hall

Zemke, R and Zemke, S (1981) '30 Things we Know for Sure About Adult Learning', in *Training the Magazine of Human Resources Development*, Vol 18, No 6, June 1981

Zimbardo, PG (1979) *Psychology and Life*, 10th edition, Illinois, Scott, Foresman and Company

Index

quantitative disciplines 124
quick fix syndrome 39

ratomorphism 30, 60
readiness to learn 49
recurrent education 26–35, 159–61
Recurrent Education 28
*Recurrent Education for Australia:
    Statement of Intent* 28
reflective observation 87
reinforcement 21, 86, 93–4
reinforcement theory 30
relationship behaviour 140
relevance in curriculum 27
relevance in education and learning 34
research 20
responsibility 22, 93–7
rote learning 23, 126

scientific method 59
self-actualisation 31, 41–3, 86, 122
self-assessment 89–90, 92
self-assurance 47
self-concept 44–7
self-confidence 47
self-control 20
self-development 91
self-directed learning 36–41
    definition 37
self-direction 46, 75, 129
self-discipline 21, 92
self-esteem 21
self-evaluation 88–9
self-identity 47, 122
self-instruction 86–8
self-leadership 129, 130
self-management 82
self-observation 83–4
self-reinforcement system 20
self-reliance 121, 122, 124

self-rewards 86
self-sufficiency 21
short-term solutions to long-term
    problems 38–9
significant learning 122
situational leadership 148–52
    application as implementation strategy
    149
    basis of 149
    in practice 152–7
situational leadership model 149
    application of 152–7
social responsibility 22
socio-emotional support 140, 143–4
stimulus response concept 21
student-centred learning 156
supervision 120
supportive behaviour 93–4

task-orientation 139–40
teacher/student relationship 45
teachers 46, 65
    role of 32, 156
    status of 42
teaching strategy 25, 46, 95
think tank 107
totalitarian man 78
trade unions 100
traditional education 46, 58, 59, 67–9,
    79
traditional environments 40
traditional learning 22, 118
training needs analysis 110
training programmes 64, 100, 102, 106,
    115
transactional analysis 38

uncertainty 59, 60

value systems 24